ANTON
CHEKHOV

A Study of the Short Fiction

Also available in Twayne's Studies in Short Fiction Series

Twayne's Studies in Short Fiction

Gordon Weaver, General Editor
Oklahoma State University

ANTON CHEKHOV
(1860–1904)
Photograph from Anton Pavlovich Chekhov: 1860–1904, *by Vladimir Yermilov*
(Moscow: Foreign Language Publishing House, n.d. [1956]).

ANTON CHEKHOV

A Study of the Short Fiction

Ronald L. Johnson

TWAYNE PUBLISHERS · _NEW YORK_
Maxwell Macmillan Canada · _Toronto_
Maxwell Macmillan International · _New York Oxford Singapore Sydney_

Twayne's Studies in Short Fiction Series, No. 40

Twayne Publishers
Macmillan Publishing Company
866 Third Avenue
New York, New York 10022

Maxwell Macmillan Canada, Inc.
1200 Eglinton Avenue East
Suite 200
Don Mills, Ontario M3C 3N1

Library of Congress Cataloging-in-Publication Data

Johnson, Ronald L.
    Anton Chekhov : a study of the short fiction / Ronald L. Johnson.
        p.   cm. — (Twayne's studies in short fiction ; no. 40)
    Includes bibliographical refernces and index.
    ISBN 0-8057-8349-0
    1. Chekhov, Anton Pavlovich, 1860–1904—Criticism and
interpretation. I. Title. II. Series.
PG3458.Z9F5347   1993
891.73′3—dc20   92-29699
                                                                 CIP

10 9 8 7 6 5 4 3 2 1

Printed in the United States of America

Contents

Preface

In the historical development of the modern short story, the importance of Anton Chekhov (1860–1904) has long been recognized: Guy de Maupassant (1850–1893) and he were the leading figures in establishing the form. Chekhov is a transitional author between nineteenth-century short fiction, which is characterized by the humorous anecdote and the romantic tale, and the modern short story, a form that enabled the literary artist to explore the nature of the individual man in the modern world. Within the development of Chekhov's own short fiction, many aspects of the rise of the modern short story can be traced. In commenting on Chekhov's importance to the short story tradition, Rufus W. Mathewson, Jr. notes that in "the dominant mode in short fiction since 1900—the casual telling of a nuclear experience in an ordinary life, rendered with immediate and telling detail—Chekhov now appears to us as chief legislator or licenser of a new and distinct way of writing."[1]

Chekhov began publishing short fiction in 1880 at the age of twenty to support his family while he was in medical school. During the next five years, he published over three hundred short items—many of them little more than jokes and anecdotes fleshed out with character types—in Moscow entertainment magazines and newspapers. And then in 1885, after he had completed his medical training, he began to develop more rapidly as a literary artist. For the next fifteen years, he continued to write short fiction, although as the quality of his stories improved, the quantity declined. Even during the remaining few years of his life, when his emphasis had shifted to drama, he wrote such prose masterpieces as "The Bishop" (1902) and "A Marriageable Girl" (1903). The chapters in Part 1 of this volume contain critical analyses of the short fiction, arranged in chronological order to provide an understanding of Chekhov's artistic development. This section begins with examples of his early apprenticeship stories, where his major themes were first sounded, and follows his progress through his mature work, with emphasis on the evolution of his technique as an artist.

One method of assessing the artistic achievement of Anton Chekhov is to consider his great influence on the modern short story. In the development of the form in the United States, England, France, and Russia, the influence of a few key writers crossed over language barriers and national boundaries. After the Constance Garnett translations of Chekhov's stories began to appear in English in 1916, his relatively plotless stories with their emphasis on mood and on the inner worlds of his characters—so unlike much of his early work—became the models for serious writers, particularly in the United States and England. Among the early twentieth-century masters of the form who recognized his genius were Sherwood Anderson (1876–1941), James Joyce (1882–1941), Virginia Woolf (1882–1941), Ernest Hemingway (1899–1961), and Katherine Mansfield (1888–1923).

Chekhov's example continues to be a significant living influence on contemporary writers of short fiction. When twenty-five contributors of a recent anthology—*The Art of the Tale: An International Anthology of Short Stories 1945-1985* (1987), edited by Daniel Halpern—were asked to name a few writers who had in some crucial way influenced their own work, Anton Chekhov appeared on the lists of ten contributors, twice as often as any other writer—Henry James (1843–1916) and James Joyce both appeared on the lists of five contributors. Among those writers who cite Chekhov as a crucial influence are V.S. Pritchett (b. 1900), Eudora Welty (b. 1909), Peter Taylor (b. 1917), Nadine Gordimer (b. 1923), Edna O'Brien (b. 1932), and Raymond Carver (1939–1988). Andre Dubus (b. 1939), another outstanding contemporary writer of short fiction, also considers Chekhov's stories to be one of the most significant literary influences in the development of his own short fiction.[2] Rufus Mathewson believes Chekhov's imprint can be discerned in the work of a range of writers from Katherine Mansfield and Sherwood Anderson through John O'Hara and Isaac Babel to Flannery O'Connor, Yurii Kazakov, and Grace Paley. In terms of specific influences, Mathewson notes Chekhov made it possible for later writers to do what they have done, "not necessarily by way of direct influence, but by setting a happy precedent that has released the creative energies of others . . . (13).

During his lifetime, Chekhov's short fiction was widely recognized in Russia. Only Leo Tolstoy (1828–1910) was better known. Of the literary giants of nineteenth-century Russia—Alexander Pushkin (1799–1837), Nikolai Gogol (1809–1852), Ivan Turgenev (1818–1883), Fyodor Dostoevsky (1821–1881), Leo Tolstoy, and Anton Chekhov—only Chekhov's reputation was founded principally on his short fiction; Pushkin, Gogol, Tolstoy, and Dostoevsky all wrote short fiction, much of it excellent, and many scholars consider the form and the sensibility of the stories in

Turgenev's *Sportsman's Sketches* (1851) as the world's first examples of the modern short story. So the tradition of Russian short fiction, which also included such prominent figures as Mikhail Lermontov (1814–1841) and Nikolai Leskov (1831–1895), was a fertile ground to nourish Chekhov's growth as an artist.

Although Chekhov is historically important, it is his artistic accomplishment that qualifies him as probably the most important figure in the short story form. The high quality of his mature work is amazing. Over fifty of his stories are termed "great" in the author's background description in a recent anthology of his work.[3] Possibly only Henry James equals his consistently high achievement in the long form of the novella. Chekhov was an equally brilliant master of the standard short story of some two thousand to fifteen thousand words—here he has no equal in terms of sheer quantity of excellent stories. And he wrote many short-short stories, stories of less than two thousand words, a number of which have been relatively ignored until the last decade or so because of the lack of critical appreciation of the form. Many of these short-short pieces are humorous early genre pieces, although he did write an occasional gem. One indication of the new interest in stories in this form is the lead story, "At Sea—A Sailor's Story," in the 1988 American collection edited by Tobias Wolff.

In 1934, thirty years after Chekhov's death, W. Somerset Maugham (1874–1965), a short story writer himself of more than passing accomplishment, noted some specific areas in Chekhov's artistic accomplishment: no one had a "greater gift than he for giving you the intimate feel of a place, a landscape, a conversation" or a character.[4] In the succeeding generations since Maugham's comments, the overall quality of the short story has generally improved, particularly in the last three decades since the demise of the large-circulation magazine market for genre stories, yet no other writer of short fiction has appeared to seriously challenge Chekhov's position. Readers not acquainted with the complete body of Chekhov's work, however, will not be aware of his great range: that intimate feel of place and landscape and character occurs in a wide variety of settings, from the cities of Moscow and St. Petersburg to provincial towns throughout European Russia to the vast estates and small farms and peasant villages of rural Russia, from the Cossack steppe country in southern Russia to the outreaches of Siberia. Accordingly, Chekhov's protagonists are drawn from all classes and walks of life; he writes of aristocrats, industrialists, small town merchants, writers and painters, religious folk and functionaries, day laborers, servants, peasants, convicts, petty thieves and murderers, even an institutionalized mental patient. Kenneth Lantz notes in his excellent essay on Chekhov's characters that there are over 8,000 different types in his work, with the vast majority of these occurring in the short fiction.[5]

Chekhov not only had a wide range of interests in terms of character and setting, he also treated a number of subjects and themes. Perhaps his most famous theme is his great belief in the freedom of the individual; he is often quoted on the subject by Russian public figures such as Andrei Sakharov and Boris Yeltsin, whose favorite author is Chekhov. Chekhov was greatly interested in human rights—in the prime of his working life he made a trip to Siberia to inspect convict conditions—and had an aversion to the "lie." In Chekhov's moral world, no lie is ever justified.

The search for a meaningful, authentic life is another aspect of his concern for the individual, and that search occupies his mature work more than any other single theme. Related to it are such concerns as the love relationships between men and women and the lack of communication among individuals, and the theme that became a hallmark of the twentieth century: the trials of hard-working and well-meaning individuals defeated by the trivial tasks and disabling boredom of modern life.

Chekhov was also vitally concerned with the nature of the human community, as it appears in the peasant village, the provincial town, or the large city. Most of Chekhov's early work features urban characters whom he satirized for the humorous newspapers of the day; in particular, he poked fun at characters obsessed with decorum, usually low-ranking public officials and bureaucrats such as Police Inspector Otchumyelov in "A Chameleon" (1894) and Sergeant Prishibeyev in the story named for him (1885). This concern was transformed in his later masterpieces into an interest in those figures who stifle individual aspirations and rights in the name of some false sense of decorum, characters such as Bilikov in "A Hard Case" (also translated as "The Man in a Case," 1898). Another important development is his treatment of peasants, which is traced in Part 1 from his earliest work to his late masterpieces.

Chekhov's reputation as a playwright, which was only established during the last few years of his life, has followed his reputation as one of the world's foremost practitioners of short fiction. For the last forty years, the critical response to his major plays—*The Seagull* (1896), *Uncle Vanya* (1900), *The Three Sisters* (1901), and *The Cherry Orchard* (1904)—has established him as one of the leading figures in the history of drama. My comments on the various connections between the subjects, themes, and characters of his short fiction and his plays are contained in the analyses of individual stories, which may be accessed through the index.

Very early in his publishing career Chekhov was striving for the objective stance toward his material that distinguishes his artistic achievement. In a 1883 letter to his brother, he terms subjectivity a "terrible thing." Objectivity for Chekhov did not mean lack of emotion, for his stories revolve around the emotional lives of his protagonists; rather, objectivity was Chekhov's idea of realism in which he strove to reveal the individual nature of the men and women of his age. Part 2 of this volume examines Chekhov's own comments on the art of writing short fiction.

The articles reprinted in Part 3 serve as an introductory guide to Chekhov criticism. The extent of the full body of critical material on Chekhov is astounding. In 1985 Kenneth Lantz limited his *Anton Chekhov: A Reference Guide to Literature* to 1200 titles, and since 1983 a number of good works have appeared. Notable recent collections of essays in English are Toby Clyman, ed., *A Chekhov Companion* (1985), and Thomas Eekman, ed., *Critical Essays on Anton Chekhov* (1989). A valuable guide for the beginning student is Charles W. Meister, *Chekhov Criticism: 1880 through 1986* (1988), which includes comments on specific stories from various critics.

I wish to thank my Chekhov students, especially Martin Achatz, for their interest and suggestions: Professors George Javor and Stewart Kingsbury; Jacquelyn Greising, Lydia M. Olson Library, Northern Michigan University, for her work in interlibrary loans; Gordon Weaver, because he knows how it gets done; Jon and Ann, for the inspiration of their presence; and, always, Sheila, fellow writer and life's fellow traveller.

A Note on the Translations

The different translations of Chekhov's stories in English present special problems for readers.[6] Since many of the stories have been translated more than once, some stories are widely known in English by more than one title. Finding a specific story, therefore, can be frustrating when searching the dozens of translations. Accordingly, an appendix at the end of the book lists the titles of the stories I have discussed, with their Russian names and any other fairly common English titles they may have. The index also lists these other English titles. A special section in the bibliography entitled "Translators" lists some useful translations of Chekhov's short stories.

Notes

1. "Chekhov's Legacy: Icebergs and Epiphanies," in *Chekhov and Our Age: Responses to Chekhov by American Writers and Scholars*, ed. James McConkey (Ithaca, New York: Cornell University, n.d.), 13. From the Chekhov and Contemporary Writing Festival 1977–1978 at Cornell University.

2. Thomas E. Kennedy, *Andre Dubus: A Study of the Short Fiction* (Boston: Twayne Publishers, 1988), 89.

3. *A Doctor's Visit: Short Stories by Anton Chekhov*, ed. Tobias Wolff (New York: Bantam, 1988).

4. W. Somerset Maugham, *East and West*, Vol. 1 of the *Complete Short Stories of W. Somerset Maugham* (Garden City, New York: Doubleday and Company, 1934), x–xiv.

5. "Chekhov's Cast of Characters," *A Chekhov Companion*, ed. Toby W. Clyman (Westport: Greenwood Press, 1985), 71.

6. The various translations of Chekhov's work in English are the subject of an excellent article by Lauren G. Leighton, "Chekhov in English" (*A Chekhov Companion*; see note 5 above), 291–309. Leighton declares that probably no other Russian writer has been as widely translated in English as Chekhov: "By widely is meant profusely—by many translators over a significant period of time, in diverse selections by chronology, length, form, type, or theme, and in numerous editions revised by both translators and editors, in accordance with the differing norms of British and American English" (291).

Acknowledgements

I gratefully acknowledge the following:

My faculty peers who recommended me for a sabbatical for Part 1 of this book; this sabbatical was arranged by Dr. John F. Kuhn, Associate Vice-President, and was funded by the Northern Michigan University Development Fund. My faculty peers who recommended me for a Northern Michigan University Faculty Grant for Part 2, which was administered through the good offices of Mr. Perrin Fenske, Director, Office of Research Development, and my English department faculty peers and Dr. Leonard Heldreth, Head, Department of English, who recommended me for released time for Part 3.

Selections for Parts 2 and 3:

Excerpts from *The Letters of Anton Chekhov* translated by Michael Henry Heim, selection and introduction by Simon Karlinsky. Copyright © 1973 by Harper & Row, Publishers, Inc. Reprinted by permission of HarperCollins Publishers.

From *The Letters of Anton Chekhov* by Anton Chekhov, translated by Avrahm Yarmolinsky, translation copyright © 1973 Avrahm Yarmolinsky. Copyright 1947, © by The Viking Press. Used by permission of Viking Penguin, a division of Penguin Books USA Inc.

Excerpts from *The Selected Letters of Anton Chekhov* edited by Lillian Hellman. Copyright © 1955 and renewal copyright © 1964 by Lillian Hellman. Reprinted by permission of Farrar, Straus and Giroux, Inc.

From: "Introduction," from *The Portable Chekhov* by Avrahm Yarmolinsky, editor. Copyright 1947, 1968 by Viking Penguin, Inc. Renewed copyright © 1975 by Avrahm Yarmolinsky. Used by permission of Viking Penguin, a division of Penguin Books USA Inc.

Part 1

THE SHORT FICTION

The Early Stories, 1880–1884

Anton Chekhov was one of the many early short story writers whose first professional publications appeared in the newspapers and weekly entertainment magazines coming into existence in the second half of the nineteenth century. These publications appeared across the Western world in response to the market created by a mass reading audience. Chekhov not only published fiction in them, but anecdotes, sketches, and local color items. During the early part of his career, Chekhov thought of himself primarily as a journalist, a writer for these weekly journals and newspapers. Almost twenty years later, looking back over his career in 1889, he listed his journalistic items as "trial reporting, reviews, miscellaneous articles, short news items," and columns.[1] For a couple of years, between 1883 and 1885, working under the constant pressure of press deadlines, he wrote a weekly column titled "Fragments of Moscow Life" for *Fragments* (*Oskolki*), one of St. Petersburg's entertainment magazines. For several generations, editors of publications like this one informally trained short story writers by providing comments and revision suggestions on their work. From such editors Chekhov first learned the essential technique of brevity, the necessary ability to portray complex material in a precise manner.

In 1880, at the age of twenty, Chekhov began writing for these publications to help support himself and his family after he enrolled as a medical student at Moscow University. At this time, Chekhov's older brother Alexander, a talented journalist, was already writing for the same editors and thus served as a model and valuable contact. Within a few short years, Chekhov was publishing regularly: in 1883 alone, he published over one hundred items, most of them short entertainment pieces. In the fiction of this period Chekhov treats a wide range of subject matter and explores a variety of forms: the anecdote, the sketch, the short-short story, the traditional short story, and the novella.

The most noteworthy of the ten items published during 1880, his first year of apprenticeship, is "Because of Little Apples" (Yarmolinsky 1954), a satiric story of some two thousand words about a landowner who catches a pair of his peasant servants—a young lad and his fiancée—

stealing apples from his orchard. The landowner orders the young woman to physically beat the young man, and then, in turn, orders the young man to beat her. The landowner threatens to have them both whipped if they do not comply. Such an outlandish situation is typical of the kind of material Chekhov handled as he made his early reputation as a humorist. But below the surface dilemma, Chekhov has created a situation with larger concerns, for the action is not without consequence: after this experience, the peasant couple end their relationship, and avoid each other. Not only is the landowner portrayed as a "beast," but his miscreant servant, nicknamed "Hangman" by the village, now accompanies him everywhere with his "maliciously grinning little mug." From the very beginning of his career, Chekhov holds up the peasant as well as the landowner as objects for his satire.

By 1883, at the age of twenty-three, Chekhov had become accomplished in the short-short story form. This form was preferred by Chekhov's editors, including Nicholas Leykin (1841–1906), editor of *Fragments*, who did more than any other editor to help Chekhov at this early stage in his career. The short-short story differs from other forms of the same length such as the anecdote and the sketch, which Chekhov also published during this period, in that the short-short story describes a significant action that generates a complexity of tone. Certainly in part it was this length requirement—against which Chekhov at times rebelled—that enabled him to develop his skill in brevity.

Years later, Chekhov assessed his contribution to the development of the short-short story and the regular short story in a comment to Ivan Bunin (1870–1958), a younger Russian writer influenced by Chekhov's stories. Chekhov related how the writer of the "little tale" is praised for his efforts, but the critics "used to scold me for it. And how they scolded." Chekhov stated that if you wished to be a writer then, you wrote novels; otherwise they wouldn't speak or listen to you and would keep you out of the important magazines. For "the sake of the miniature story, I broke my head against a wall on your behalf."[2]

A typical early story is "A Slander" (Garnett). A school teacher stops by the kitchen to watch his cook bake sturgeon for the the wedding reception of the schoolteacher's daughter. Relishing the delectable smell of the fish, the schoolteacher kisses his fingertips. The smacking sound is heard in the next room, and one of the guests declares the cook is smooching with someone. When the guest then discovers the schoolteacher with the cook, he teasingly accuses the schoolteacher. The story develops as the schoolteacher overreacts in his attempts to deny the accusation he kissed the cook. The more the schoolteacher denies, the more quickly the rumor spreads, until both his superior at school and his wife accuse him of a sexual affair with the cook. The story closes with the schoolteacher recognizing that in fact the guest who had seen him with the cook had not spread the rumor. As the schoolteacher desperately searches his mind wondering who did so, the reader realizes that the efforts of the schoolteacher himself to squelch the rumor have created the problem. Here Chekhov employs the traditional device of comic reversal: the result of the action is the direct opposite of the character's intentions.

With just such a tale as this, Leykin, the editor at *Fragments*, was most pleased. Leykin, who wrote humor pieces himself, wanted to entertain his readers. Chekhov, however, differed in one important aspect from most other contributors: he also wanted to write to explore the deeper sides of life, to protest seriously against the inhuman behavior of the people he saw about him. This impulse is obvious in one of Chekhov's best short-short stories, a masterpiece of the form, "At Sea—A Sailor's Story" (Dunnigan), narrated by a young sailor on a ship with passenger cabins. He and another sailor had carved two peepholes in the honeymoon cabin. As the action opens, on a night that threatens rain, the crew are casting lots to determine who will use the peepholes later that evening. The young sailor comments that a sailor can be the foulest of creatures on the earth, "fouler than the lowest beast" (33); he declares "We sailors . . . are dissolute because we do not know what one needs virtue for at sea" (34). This comment recalls the moral trials of the sailor narrators of Joseph Conrad (1857–1924).

The young sailor wins the casting of the lots along with his father, an old humpbacked sailor who declares, "Today, my boy, we're lucky! . . . Luck came to us both at the same time. That means something" (34). The true nature of that luck unfolds as the scene develops. Through his peephole the narrator observes the young bridegroom, a pastor, and his beautiful bride talking to a middle-aged, gaunt Englishwoman and her plump banker husband. After the middle-aged couple leaves, the pastor argues with his bride about something that the two eavesdroppers cannot hear. At first the woman shakes her head in refusal, but then, after the supplications of the groom—during which her face shows anger and inner struggle—she consents. The groom leaves and then returns with the plump Englishman, who goes to the bed and asks the bride a question. When she nods her head in affirmation, the banker pulls a wad of money from his pocket, and hands it to the groom, who leaves.

As the banker locks the door, the narrator springs away from the peephole as if he were stung. He feels frightened, and his father, that "drunken, debauched old man," takes the narrator's arm and leads him away, declaring, "You shouldn't see that. You're still a boy" (36). The irony is complete; the sailor who considered himself without virtue is outraged at the actions of people who would consider themselves his moral superior. As the story closes, the narrator and his father stumble up the stairs toward deck, where the rain is now falling, providing closure to the story.

Another outstanding short-short story from the same year is "A Daughter of Albion" (Garnett), a more subtle story than "At Sea." A local official, Otsov, stops by a neighbor's estate for a drink and finds the landowner, Gryabov, out fishing with his English governess. A large stout man, Gryabov sits with "his legs tucked under him like a Turk." Beside him stands the thin Englishwoman, with "prominent eyes like a crab's and a big birdlike nose more like a hook than a nose" (XIII, 217). She is dressed in a white muslin gown through which her "scraggy yellow shoulders were very distinctly apparent" (XIII, 217). These sharply observed details, along with the witty and exact dialogue, make the story effective.

The complexity of the situation develops when Gryabov calls the Englishwoman—who remains standing beside him, without knowledge of Russian—a "she-devil," whose "nose alone is enough to make one faint." Otsov declares he is uncomfortable with Gryabov's remarks, but Gryabov goes on to term her an "ugly doll" who smells of "something decaying." When Gryabov snags his hook, he decides to undress so he will not wet his clothes when he wades in to free it. He motions for the Englishwoman to go down the bank and hide behind some bushes, but she refuses. When Gryabov begins to undress anyway, Otsov protests his action is "outrageous, an insult." But Gryabov replies it is "a lesson for these foreigners" and strips until he is "in the costume of Adam." The woman smiles disdainfully, puts another worm on her hook, yawns, and drops the hook in the water.

Maxim Gorky (1868–1936) referred to this story in his comment on Chekhov's writing: "The esteemed public reading 'A Daughter of Albion' laughs over it, without probably seeing in this story the odious mockery of a lonely person, to whom all and everything are alien, by a well-fed gentleman." In every one of Chekhov's humorous stories

Gorky could detect the "low deep sigh of a pure and truly human heart"; he believed nobody had ever understood "the tragedy of life's trifles so subtly and penetratingly as Anton Chekhov," for "nobody has ever revealed to his fellow creatures so ruthlessly and fairly, the shameful, dismal picture of their lives in the murky chaos of commonplace vulgarity."[3]

In commenting on Chekhov's achievement in his short-short stories, Vladimir Yermilov notes Chekhov became "the creator of a new form of literature—the very short story" and the restrictions that had "at first caused him such suffering—the necessity for ruthless cutting, erasing, rejecting—was now converted into an artistic tenet," one which stressed brevity. Certainly Chekhov, who declared he had learned how to "talk briefly about big things" (Yermilov, 54), was aware of his importance in establishing the form (Yermilov, 105).

Chekhov's best-known subject for these miniature tales was the Russian civil service bureaucrat. The "little man" in that bureaucracy had long been a tradition in Russian literature, "The Overcoat" (1842) by Nikolai Gogol (1809–1852) being the most famous example. Chekhov's satiric treatment of the lowly clerk who fawns before his office superior became popular with the readers of entertainment papers, many of them civil servants themselves. "Two in One" (Yarmolinsky 1954) is a typical example. A civil service official, riding a streetcar, observes one of his clerks ordering people about. But when the clerk recognizes the official, the clerk undergoes a physical transformation: "Instantly his back curved, his face fell, his voice died away, his arms stiffened along the seams of his trousers, he sagged at the knees" (35). After the clerk hides his nose in his collar, the official marvels that this "crestfallen, flattened mannikin" should have had such a presence before he was recognized. That physical transformation from an upright person to a shrunken, fawning subordinate whenever a superior appears is a common occurrence in these stories of the bureaucracy.

One of Chekhov's most widely known stories of the relationship between officials and their clerks, this one told from the viewpoint of the subordinate, is "The Death of a Civil Servant" (Miles). Ivan is attending the opera when he uncontrollably sneezes, splattering the bald head of a high-ranking official sitting in front of him. Although this man is not his immediate superior, Ivan apologizes during the intermission and attempts to explain that his action was not planned. The high-ranking official brushes off the apology, and Ivan goes home, where he worries about the incident until he decides to go to the official's home to explain himself further. There the official again brushes him off, asking Ivan if he is attempting to make fun of him. The comedy develops from the same reversal of intentions described in "A Slander." Ivan, worried that the official now believes the worst, goes once again to his home in an attempt to explain. The official loses his temper and shouts at Ivan, demanding that Ivan "Clear out!" Ivan is so upset he goes home, lies down on his couch, and dies.

The times and settings of Chekhov's early stories for the weekly papers were often suggested by the approach of a holiday: Christmas, New Year's, Shrovetide, Easter, or a saint's day, particularly St. Peter's Day. For his Shrovetide story in 1883, he used the feast of an office chief for one of his most satiric stories. In "The Conqueror's Triumph" (Jones) the narrator is the son of one of the chief's clerks. After the feasting, the chief relates how as a young clerk himself, he was persecuted by one of the old clerks now at the feast. The chief suddenly orders the old clerk to put some pepper on a piece of bread and eat it. When the old clerk, already stuffed from the feasting, immediately does so, eating the whole thing, the company shrieks in laughter. Then the chief orders the narrator and his father—who wishes to secure a position for the narrator—to run around the table and to crow like roosters: "My papa smiled, blushed with pleasure, and took several quick little steps around the table. I followed. 'Cock-a-doodle do!' we both shouted and ran faster. And I was thinking as I ran, 'I am going to be an assistant clerk!'" (98–99). The humor of this vaudeville-like activity—which suggests the early playwright in Chekhov—underscores the debasement of the clerks, satirizing behavior and begging the question: Is this the way free men should behave?

The question was one that Chekhov continued to work through in his fiction. For his New Year's story in 1884, "The Liberal—A New Year's Day Story" (Jones), Chekhov depicts a different type of clerk than those in "The Conqueror's Triumph." This clerk makes the traditional annual visit to his superior's home, where he refuses to perform an imitation of a steam engine, which the chief inadvertently had seen him doing at the office. When the chief voices his disappointment, the clerk becomes frightened at the potential result of his refusal. The ambivalence of this clerk reflects a current concern of Chekhov's: the behavior of the "slave." In a letter of 1889, Chekhov remarks that one might describe him as a young man who has "played the hypocrite both to God and man without any need but merely out of the consciousness of his own insignificance." Chekhov believed that, as a young man, he squeezed "the slave out of himself drop by drop," so that "awakening one fine morning," he felt "running in his veins no longer the blood of a slave but genuine human blood." As a writer, he required most of all a "sense of personal freedom," and "it was only recently that that sense began blazing up within me."[4]

In contrast to the short-short story, which often centers on one scene, other early stories look toward the longer, more traditional form of the story with its sequence of events over time leading to a climax. This form, which often runs to eight or nine thousand words or more, took Chekhov longer to master. An early example is "St. Peter's Day," (Payne), a farcical entertainment about a shooting party on the opening day of hunting season. Although the action holds the reader's interest, the sequence of events is related in a confusing manner, and the story is obviously an apprentice's effort. In order to chart the development of this longer form, this story can be compared to Chekhov's story of the opening of hunting season written one year later, in 1882, "The Twenty-ninth of June" (Smith). In this story, a little over one half as long, the change in point of view from the omniscient narrator of "St. Peter's Day" to the first-person narrator who participates in the hunt focuses the sequence of events and creates a much tighter form.

Another early story contains a subject that was to become another important concern for the mature Chekhov: love. "Green Scythe" (Payne) is subtitled "A Short Novel." The subtitle is more a comment on the subject of love in the story than on its genre, for its form is most definitely that of the traditional short story. Although it lacks the artistic depth of Chekhov's later work, it is a well-made, light entertainment.

Chekhov also explores the subject of love in "A Living Chattel" (Garnett). Although this novella, some twelve thousand words long, is clumsily constructed, and although the characters remain stereotyped, its treatment of the circumstances of adultery and of the power of love is a first step toward such later masterpieces as "A Lady with a Dog." It is a reminder that Chekhov achieved such masterpieces only through working the same theme through several stories. In "A Living Chattel," a wealthy landowner, Groholsky, has fallen in love with an attractive young woman, Liza. Unfortunately, she is married to a poor clerk, Bugrov, so Groholsky convinces Bugrov to give up Liza for a large sum of money. Although Chekhov does not yet have the ability to explore the moral implications of a man's selling his wife, he does offer significant insight into the relationship between the sexes. The portrayal of the woman as living merchandise is complex: Liza is bought and sold, but the husband, not she, is morally degraded. The grandson of a former serf, Chekhov was sensitive to the moral complications of one person's owning another, even if he could not yet fully explore them.

Chekhov also explores that subject of owning humans in "The Lady of the Manor" (Jones), an eight thousand word story published the same month as "A Living Chattel." This story goes beyond the light entertainment of a piece like "Green Scythe" to a seriousness of moral purpose that was first sounded in "Because of Little Apples." In this story Chekhov also seriously began exploring characters of the peasant class, the class that provided him with protagonists in his short fiction for the remainder of his life. In "The Lady of the Manor," the baroness lusts after one of the young peasants on her estate, Stepan, who lives with his pregnant wife in his parents' hut. Stepan has left his job as coachman after an initial sexual advance by the baroness and come home to his parents' hut. He does not want to return to the manor for to do so would lead to sin. The story moves according to the logic of the Naturalist school although Chekhov did not consciously subscribe to the tenets of the contemporary European literary movement led by Emile Zola (1840–1902). When the baroness drives by the hut and demands Stepan come back, his brother and his father insist that he go. His father reminds Stepan that Stepan needs the help of the baroness to build a place for himself.

Although the serfs had been legally emancipated for twenty years when this story was written, economically the vast majority remained tied to the large estates, and many faced a difficult situation without the goodwill of the landowners. (Such peasants were in a position similar to the black sharecropper in the American South after the Civil War: technically, they were free, but to prosper—or even simply to survive—many were dependent on the economic goodwill of the former master.) Stepan's wife, Marya, pleads with him not to go, and he tells her he will not. But after a beating from his father for not going—which Stepan takes as a dutiful peasant son—he returns to the baroness. He tells the baroness he will comply with her wishes on the condition his father and brother do not benefit. When Stepan's brother and his father attempt to gain from Stepan's situation, the baroness remains true to Stepan's one wish and does not allow it. In retaliation, Stepan's wife is thrown out of his parents' hut.

The next morning, a Sunday appropriately enough, Stepan returns to the village, stopping by the tavern, where he becomes involved in a fierce fight with his brother and the village deacon. Stepan flees the crowd that chases him. To his great relief, he finds Marya, and begs her to flee the country with him. Marya, however, accuses Stepan of ruining her life. As she shouts at him, he blindly doubles up his fist and hits her with all his strength, killing her. The story ends with the baroness's horror when she learns of this action, declaring, "'Those terrible peasants! . . . Oh, how terrible they are! The wretches!'" (130). Although both the baroness and the peasants remain two-dimensional figures, individual scenes in the story are powerful. Chekhov's moral position is well-defined. As in "Because of Little Apples," the landowner may be at fault, but the peasant is not without blame: the baroness may be the antagonist in the story, but Stepan's brother and father are as morally reprehensible as she. Although many critics believe it is a mistake to view Chekhov as a political progressive, charting the decay of Imperial Russia in his works, certainly in such an early story as "The Lady of the Manor," the twenty-two year old Chekhov did not hesitate to call attention to faults in the structure of his society as well as aberrations in its people.

Chekhov explored the subject of the relationship between the landowner and the peasant in a number of other stories from this period such as "Trifon" (Jones) and "In the Home for the Senile and Incurably Ill" (Miller). In these stories, landowners yearn for the unbridled power they held over the serfs in the days before the Emancipation, a situation which resembles the slave-holding, antebellum days of the American South. But it is not always the landowners who yearn for the past. In "The Retired Slave" (Smith), an old peasant is nostalgic for the experiences he had living with his former master. Chekhov's most famous former serf who yearns for the past, Firs, comes not from his short fiction, but from his play *The Cherry Orchard* (1904).

Although these stories on the subject of the landowner and peasant have interest for their content, they do not display the artistic achievement of "He Understood" (Dunnigan), which Donald Rayfield terms the most substantial and mature of the over one hundred pieces Chekhov published in 1883.[5] The peasant in this story, who has been caught hunting before the season opens, is brought before the landowner and upbraided for shooting a starling. The landowner sends for the constable to bring charges, but the sly peasant, who knows the landowner is an alcoholic, explains that his desire to hunt is an "illness." He declares that, like an alcoholic, he cannot keep himself from hunting, and describes the experience in vivid detail. After this explanation, the landowner "did understand—not from kindness, but from experience," and allows the peasant to go free. As in "At Sea," written within a short time of "He Understood," Chekhov employs the technique of foreshadowing: a rain that threatens at the opening of the story finally falls at the close as the peasant leaves the house, providing a sense of ending to the story.

A few months after the publication of "A Living Chattel," Chekhov published another novella, "Late-Blooming Flowers" (Chertok), which marks an artistic improvement in terms of character development and narrative pacing. The longer form of short fiction, the novella, was more difficult than any other for Chekhov to master. It would him take another half dozen years to do so, but eventually it would become one of his favored forms.[6] As in "A Living Chattel," the subject of "Late-Blooming Flowers" is the relationship between the sexes. The two main characters are the attractive young woman who yearns for fulfillment through love and the hard-working doctor, figures who were to become mainstays of Chekhov's later work. The young woman is a member of an aristocratic family, and the doctor is a son of her dead father's valet. The doctor treats her for pneumonia, and she falls in love with him, admiring what she believes is his great strength of character. Despite his industriousness, he is not the ideal doctor she believes, but rather a man who has placed social position and money above helping the sick. The inauthentic life he leads and the toll that life exacts from him look forward to the protagonists of Chekhov's later masterpieces.

In this early period, a number of other, shorter stories also explore the relationship between the sexes in various tones, although none displays the depth of character of "Late-Blooming Flowers." The parody of "An Enigmatic Nature" (Garnett) is primarily aimed at the admirers of the Dostoevskian heroine of suffering. A more accomplished story, full of Chekhov's delightful humor, is "The Woman Who Had No Prejudices—A Romance" (Jones). A man of great physical strength is desperately in love with a woman from a higher social class, but he is afraid she will not marry him. When she agrees, he waits until the wedding night to tell of his past, for fear of rejection. When he tells her that as a child he sold fruit on the streets like a beggar, she is surprised, but not disapproving, so then he tells his darkest secret: as a young man of twenty he performed as a clown in the circus. The bride jumps up and runs around the room in laughter. Covering the groom with kisses, she demands he perform some trick to prove he indeed was a clown, so he does a handstand on the bed and begins to walk around the room on his hands. When the bride's father goes to the room the next morning, he discovers the groom performing somersaults in the air with the bride applauding, and "both of their faces were shining with joy" (51).

This vaudevillelike action looks forward to Chekhov's early one-act plays.[7] During this period Chekhov wrote not only journalistic reviews of theater productions, but also a number of sketches and stories on the subject of the theater, and his first book, *Tales of Melpomene* (1884), is a small collection of theater stories. The better stories on the subject during this period are "The Baron" and "In the Graveyard." In "The Baron" (Jones), the love of a decrepit old prompter for *Hamlet* causes him to be dismissed, with the humor arising from his attitude toward the failings of the other actors in his company. The humor of "In the Graveyard" (Garnett) is more subtle, with a tinge of the bittersweet. A group of men at the graveyard are approached by a nondescript actor searching for the grave of a fellow actor. The actor claims he shall never forget the dead actor, because that man inspired him to become an actor himself. Now, however, this actor is ruined, destitute, and alcoholic; the doctors say he will soon die. Chekhov himself attended plays regularly, and continued to write fiction about theater people, especially during the next half-dozen years. Later in life, he married a famous actress, Olga Knipper, who starred in his own plays, which he often helped to stage.

One of the most frequent modes for Chekhov's humor was the parody, whether of a popular attitude, as in "An Enigmatic Nature," or of the popular genre stories of the day. In "The Sinner from Toledo—A Translation from the Spanish" (Hinchcliffe), a melodramatic parody of the Gothic romance of the Spanish Inquisition, a man poisons his wife because she has been accused of witchcraft, and the husband believes he will receive absolution for his sins because he has killed a witch.

Chekhov would turn to the Gothic tale as the subject of a folktale retold in "The Bet" (Garnett) and as the subject for exploration of the mystical in a masterpiece, "The Black Monk." But in general, his sensibility lay out of the Gothic and the supernatural, the elements that help shape the form of short fiction termed the "tale" by critics. Instead, Chekhov leaned toward realism, which became the grounds for the development of the modern short story.

Chekhov's realism from this early period took two forms: comic realism and the traditional serious realism of the age. For generations, the average Russian reader viewed Chekhov as a primarily comic writer.

One direction for his comedy was in genre parody, as in "The Sinner From Toledo" and "The Swedish Match—A Murder Story" (Garnett), a more sophisticated parody on the genre of the detective story. He also increasingly focused on character, as displayed in two stories published within five weeks of each other in 1884, where his comic characters are at their best. Gradusov, the protagonist in "Worse and Worse" (Yarmolinsky 1954), is a precursor for the famous Sergeant Prishibeyev in the story by that title published a year later. Gradusov, an old irascible, opinionated leader of the church choir has insulted one of its members, and a lawyer persuades him to publicly apologize. But in a series of court proceedings, Gradusov not only insults the choir member again and slaps him, but also insults the court officials and his own lawyer. Gradusov's dialogue provides the humor in the story and defines his character. There is enough truth in his obstinate behavior, and in his rationalization for that behavior, to fix his character as a type in the manner of the characters of Theophrastus (4th century B.C.), who are defined not by their professions, but by how their behavior violates the standards of good manners.

Delightful dialogue also creates the character in the second story, "A Chameleon" (Garnett). Otchumyelov, a police official, must handle the complaint of a man who has been bitten on the finger by a white borzoi puppy. The story is mostly dialogue (so we experience these characters almost as if they were actors on a stage) exchanged among the two men and a gathering crowd. Otchumyelov's reverence for rank, his outstanding trait, is the focus of Chekhov's satire, as in the stories of the bureaucratic clerks, such as "The Death of a Civil Servant." The comedy works as it does in the stories and novels of Nikolai Gogol and Charles Dickens (1812–1870), with the characters becoming caricatures.

The situation in "Oysters" (Garnett) contains elements of comedy, but of a different kind—the comic pathos of Dickens, where "tears through the laughter" is the mode, comes to mind. This tears and laughter theme has a long tradition in Russian society, where the sense of humor is darker than its American counterpart, meaning that a Russian may be able to find humor in situations where a Westerner would likely see only tragedy. This ability is evident in Chekhov's short stories, and sometimes aided by Chekhov's giving the reader direct access to the minds of the characters, so we see the world from their perspective. In "Oysters," the narrator recounts an experience from his childhood in which he and his father were destitute and went begging in the streets of Moscow. The narrator, who is starving to death, begins to lose touch with reality. Reading the word "Oysters" on a restaurant wall, the narrator, who has never seen oysters, imagines what they must be like, and in his disoriented state, cries out, "Oysters! Give me some oysters!" (61). Two gentlemen overhear his cry, and amused at this strange request, take the boy into the restaurant where he eats his fill. Chekhov was proud of this story in that he felt he had successfully used his medical knowledge to create the psychological state of a person starving to death. But in portraying this character, Chekhov not only generates the psychological reality as he creates the comic situation, but exposes the suffering of urban poverty. The last image of the story is of the father walking up and down the street the next day, gesticulating as he mutters to himself, preparing to beg. The seriousness of the tone sets the laughter in a different context, one which invites the reader to sympathize with the character as well as to laugh at his foibles.

The direction toward serious realism was to be Chekhov's main line of development in his mature period. One such realistic portrayal of character from this early period is found in "The Thief" (Smith), in which Chekhov explores the psychological state of an unsympathetic convict exiled to Siberia. This story was written seven years before Chekhov's trip to Siberia in 1890.

"In the Autumn" (Smith), perhaps the most haunting realistic story Chekhov wrote during this period, is another exploration of suffering, without the humor that relieves the situation as in "Oysters." A destitute alcoholic appears in a wayside tavern where pilgrims and cabdrivers have taken refuge from an autumn storm. A former landowner, the alcoholic begs the tavern owner for a drink to relieve his physical and mental suffering. Chekhov's achievement in this story is in portraying the suffering of the alcoholic and the other characters' response to his suffering without the story becoming sentimental.[8]

Chekhov was aware of the danger of such a subject, and in advising a fellow writer, he cautioned that the only way such a situation could be handled was by remaining "coldly" objective: "When you depict sad or unlucky people, and want to touch the reader's heart, try to be colder—it gives their grief as it were a background, against which it stands out in greater relief."[9] A short time afterwards, he clarified this statement by noting: "The more objective the telling, the more powerful the effect produced."[10]

In the next three years, from 1885 through 1887, Chekhov would transform the subjects that he had first explored in these early stories into some of the most outstanding work written in the history of short fiction. However, as the artist emerged, some of the more charming characteristics of these early stories—the vaudeville-like antics of the characters, the tongue-in-cheek humor—would be lost.

The Artist Emerges, 1885–1887

In the three-year period from 1885 to 1887, between the ages of twenty-five to twenty-eight, Chekhov made the transition from being primarily a writer of comic entertainment to a serious artist who wrote, not parody and comic sketches, but realistic stories about a wide range of subjects. Some of these stories—such masterpieces as "Misery," "Easter Eve," and "The Kiss"—are now commonly anthologized. Stories such as these not only marked a breakthrough in Russian literature in terms of form and conciseness, but also set the standard in literature for what was to become the traditional form of the short story. In his study of Chekhov's fiction, Karl Kramer aptly terms this traditional form one of "moral revelation," a concept that, as Kramer notes, Northrop Frye uses in conjunction with his analysis of the development of the realistic novel (Kramer, 11–27). It is easy to undervalue Chekhov's development of artistic techniques in these stories since they have become so common-place in stories by subsequent writers.

With Chekhov's increasing interest in the serious realistic story came an expansion in his publishing outlets, with new editors in turn spurring him on in this direction. His stories not only became more realistic, but he was allowed more length, until he was regularly writing stories of three to six thousand words, often more. This transition was not abrupt, but gradual. Chekhov continued to contribute pieces regularly to the entertainment magazines until late in 1887, although by January of that year, he was disgusted with the entertainment magazine and wanted "to turn out something bigger, or not write at all" (Yarmolinsky, 44).

One of the more important events in changing Chekhov's attitude toward writing serious fiction during this period was a letter he received from Dmitry Grigorovich (1822–1899), a literary lion of the age. In 1886, Grigorovich wrote a letter in response to the more serious stories Chekhov was publishing, in particular to "The Huntsman," in which he termed Chekhov a major talent and urged him to abandon his practice of working toward a press deadline so he could commit himself more completely to his stories. In his reply, Chekhov pledged to change his approach to writing, to commit himself as a literary artist. Chekhov vowed to spend more time with his stories, instead of simply dashing them off and sending them to an editor. Although he could not immediately change his working habits for financial reasons, gradually he positioned himself to attempt more ambitious work with deliberate care.

Stories of Comedy

One method of tracking Chekhov's evolution as an artist during this period is to examine his humorous stories.[11] In October of 1885 Chekhov published one of his last—and one of his best—caricatures, "Sergeant Prishibeyev" (Miles). This story portrays a shrivelled little sergeant brought before a justice of the peace for attempting to discipline the members of a village without the delegated authority to do so. Like the protagonists in "A Chameleon" and "Worse and Worse," Prishibeyev is created primarily through his dialogue. The character is famous because in Russian society Prishibeyev came to represent the man who is a slave to authority and who attempts to make others behave as he does.

Chekhov shifted his emphasis from caricature to realistic situation comedy early in this period, often using a reversal to create the humor. Such a comic plot reversal occurs in what Ronald Hingley believes is the best of all the comic stories, "The Orator" (Garnett.)[12] A man who loves to give long and eloquent speeches learns in the middle of a funeral oration he has mistaken the deceased for another man, for the supposedly deceased man is now standing before him in the crowd.

Although the comic situation stories are of uneven quality—many, in fact, are not equal to the robust intensity of the earlier caricature sketches—they chart Chekhov's shift toward a realist sensibility. Many of such comic stories have domestic settings. Typical examples are "Moral Superiority" (FitzLyon) and "In the Dark" (Garnett). In "Moral Superiority" a young groom, although ashamed of his relatives, takes his bride to visit them, with the reversal occurring when he learns his bride has the same feeling of shame about her own relatives. In "In the Dark" a wife wakes her husband in fear she's heard a burglar, but the husband learns that instead of a burglar, the cook is sneaking her lover into the house. These are the kinds of plots that reappeared in television situation comedies—"sitcoms"—in twentieth-century America in response to the same public demand that the entertainment magazines satisfied in Moscow during this period.

In contrast to the numerous short-short stories Chekhov wrote in this period is a leisurely paced story of ten thousand words, "The Privy

Councillor" (Garnett), arguably his best to date. The events are narrated from a boy's point of view; its tongue-in-cheek evaluations of the behavior of adults recalls such boyhood characters of Mark Twain (1835–1910) as Tom Sawyer and Huckleberry Finn. The family on a provincial estate has high expectations of the visit of an uncle who has distinguished himself in the larger world, but those expectations are not met in a comic reversal that results in an education for the young narrator.

Another of the better stories in this genre is "Nerves" (Garnett). Actually, "Nerves" is a parody of two genres: the domestic situation comedy and the gothic tale. A man who returns home from a seance is terribly frightened at the thought of ghosts, so he seeks the company of the maid in the middle of the night. Since the man's wife is out of the house at an all-night church service, the maid assumes the man is seeking sexual favors, and will not allow him into her room. Later, when she is asleep, the man finally makes his way into the maid's room, falls asleep, and, in a characteristic Chekhovian reversal, is discovered there the next morning by his wife.

A number of stories that treat adultery in a humorous manner comprise a subgroup of these domestic stories. Adultery was a common subject of the entertainment magazines of the day. In contrast to Chekhov's serious stories on the subject of adultery, which was to become one of his major concerns during this period, these humorous stories are relatively short, most often around two thousand words. A typical example is "An Avenger" (Garnett), in which an outraged husband goes to a gun shop to purchase a revolver to kill his wife, her lover, and then himself. But in discussing the various revolvers with the shopkeeper, the husband by stages abandons his plan, and in the end to cover the awkwardness of his position, buys a net for catching quails.

In more significant stories from this period, the humor evolves from the situation of the characters, but as in "Oysters," a touch of pathos adds dimension to the events. The young attractive woman in "A Gentleman Friend" (Garnett) has just been released from the hospital. Since she is without money, she seeks a gentleman friend to help her buy clothes so that she can attract the favors of other men. The man to whom she applies for help, a dentist, mistakenly assumes in a comic reversal that she needs a tooth extracted, so he pulls one. Pathos develops as the young woman walks along the street, spitting blood and suddenly ashamed of her profession. She broods "on her life, her ugly wretched life, and the insults she had endured, and would have to endure tomorrow, and next week, and all her life, up to the day of her death" (X, 283).

Chekhov does not end the story here, however, but returns to the comic tone as he concludes with the information that despite her momentary shame, the next day the woman was at a dance hall, dressed fashionably and attracting young men.

Another story in this tragicomic vein is "Drowning" (Yarmolinsky 1954), in which an alcoholic derelict impersonates a drowning man for money. The derelict has already figuratively drowned, submerged and obscured in the lower depths of his society. These tragicomic stories were transitional for Chekhov as he gradually abandoned a purely humorous approach to his material.

The story that best characterizes Chekhov's changing approach to humor during this period is "A Joke" (Garnett). A seemingly inconsequential little joke becomes a shaping force in a character's life, her most beautiful memory. By shifting from a whimsical to a serious tone as the story evolves, Chekhov develops a means to explore the larger issues which were to occupy many of his mature stories. These issues often arise from what appear to be the insignificant moments of one's life. The first-person narrator of "The Joke" recalls that during his young manhood he persuaded a young woman who cared very much for him to ride a sled down a dangerous, icy hill despite her great dread. At the moment when they hardly had strength enough to breathe from the pressure of the wind tearing past their faces, he whispered, "I love you." The woman could not tell whether she imagined the words or whether the narrator did, in fact, speak them. Despite her great fear, she was so consumed by her desire to know that she asked the narrator to take her down the hill again, but she still could not determine if he were truly whispering the words. She repeated her request over a period of weeks that winter, without ever learning the answer.

When spring came, the narrator, hidden by a fence that encircled the yard of the young woman, saw her come out of her house on a windy day. Waiting for a gust of wind, he repeated the words, and the young woman "uttered a cry, smiled all over her face and looking joyful, happy and beautiful, held out her arms to meet the wind" (XIII, 256). In the conclusion, the narrator relates that she has married a minor official and now has three children, but those words for her were the "happiest, most touching, and most beautiful memory in her life" (XIII, 257). The narrator, however, remains puzzled about his own motive.

The narrator here is a precursor of later characters—like the protagonist in "All Friends Together," the masterpiece that Chekhov wrote toward the end of his life—who look back upon some apparently small moment or moments that become very important, often determining the direction of a life. The Irish writer William Trevor (b. 1928) notes that in Chekhov "all human sentiment however humble its manifestation, is worthy of investigation." In commenting on Chekhov's influence, Trevor states "after Chekhov, the short story at its best reflected a view of life in which the mundane and what appeared to be the inconsequential never ceased to matter."[13]

Stories of Domestic Life and Family Relationships

In Chekhov's serious stories of domestic life, in which he evaluates the daily lives of ordinary people, he converts the mundane into the consequential. One of his better stories about domestic life, "Not Wanted" (Garnett), explores the plight of the commuter husband. During the summer months, it was fashionable for middle-class people to take summer homes a few hours outside of Moscow. Here the wife and children stayed, and the husband commuted by train from his job in the city two or three times a week. In its events, its tone, and its portrayal of the men's attitudes toward their families, their frustrations, and their belief the commute is finally worthwhile, this story resembles the Shady Hill commuter stories of John Cheever (1912–1982).

The sympathetic father in "Home" (Garnett), another domestic story of this period, resembles the middle-class protagonist in "Not Wanted." Bykovsky, a prosecutor, returns home one evening to learn from his governess that his seven-year-old son has been discovered smoking. Following the father's thoughts as he attempts to convince his son not to smoke by telling him a series of stories, Chekhov creates one of his most artistically successful stories of the relationship between a father and son. "Home" also contains Bykovsky's ideas about narrating a story, ideas that parallel Chekhov's own narrative poetics. In his bedtime stories, Bykovsky prefers to fabricate his own narrative rather than retelling established stories, so when he begins a story, he has no "notion" of how the story will develop nor how it will end: "Scenes, characters, and situations were taken at random, impromptu" in the telling, and "the plot and the moral came of itself as it were, with no plan on the part of the story teller" (XII, 76). This comment on the narrative process is of interest because Chekhov himself relied primarily on intuition in composing his stories. Bykovsky notices that "the simple and less ingenious the plot, the stronger impression it made upon their child," a statement that also applies to Chekhov's work: it was during this period he moved away from the complex, plot-oriented stories toward simpler, mood-dominated stories, such as "Not Wanted" and "Home." The story closes with Bykovsky's musing that for all his formal learning, he realizes "how he had gathered an understanding of life not from his sermons and laws, but from fables, novels, poems" (XII, 78). For Bykovsky, as for his creator, certain knowledge is best conveyed through narratives involving "scenes, characters, situations."

Other domestic stories that focus on the relationship between father and son are "A Father" and "Difficult People," an early masterpiece. In "A Father" (Garnett) a widower, an alcoholic living with a woman, sponges off his saintlike son in a series of scenes that recall the tortured familial relationships in some works of Fyodor Dostoevsky. In contrast, the violent emotions of the farmer family in "Difficult People" (Garnett) resemble those of Chekhov's own peasant characters. The oldest son, Pyotr, who has begun studying at the university in Moscow, needs money to return to school after summer vacation. But his tight-fisted father resents parting with the necessary funds. At the supper table, a fierce argument develops, and Pyotr leaves for a long walk over the steppe, which is portrayed in dismal autumnal detail that reflects his inner emotional state. When Pyotr returns home, the argument flares up again, and Pyotr loses control. Both father and son then verbally attack the mother, and they lie awake all night in that vague pain that results from family feuding. As Pyotr lies there, he does not blame anyone, but realizes that "every one in the house was feeling that same ache" (V, 84). The next morning, in a "cold hateful rain," Pyotr leaves for the station.[14]

Although the family relationships in "Difficult People" are strained, the family remains functional, mutually sharing that "ache." As difficult as that situation is, the situation in "Volodya" (Garnett) is more desperate. Volodya, a seventeen-year-old adolescent, lives with his mother and feels ashamed of her. His mother has gone through two fortunes, her own and her husband's, but Volodya does not fault her primarily for that; he detests her for making him accompany her on her visits to acquaintances of high rank. The events of the story occur largely during the course of one such visit. At a wealthy relative's villa, Volodya is seduced by a thirty-year-old married woman, who afterwards looks at him with disgust and calls him a "wretched ugly duckling." Volodya, shy and at that awkward stage of adolescence, later looks in the mirror and accepts her opinion. When Volodya returns home, he shoots himself.

Another story that culminates in the death of a young person is

"Typhus" (Garnett), which is often linked with "Oysters" and "Sleepy" in that each is concerned with the portrayal of an abnormal state of mind. A young lieutenant traveling home to Moscow is unaware he is coming down with typhoid fever. The achievement of the story is in the prose, which recreates the distorted sensations of the feverish mind of the protagonist. At home, the lieutenant is put to bed, where he passes in and out of consciousness, hallucinating, until the fever finally breaks. But after the lieutenant recovers, he learns his beloved younger sister had caught typhus from him and died, and his joy at surviving gives way to the feeling of "irrevocable loss" (302).

"Excellent People" (Garnett), a more complex story based on the relationship between a brother and a sister, is narrated by a friend of the brother. The situation is similar to that in "Typhus"; the sister, a young doctor, catches typhoid fever from her husband. When she recovers, she learns her husband has died from the illness. The sister then moves in with her brother, and the two of them grow quite close. The sister's relationship with her brother changes, however, when she becomes interested in "liberal" ideas, in particular in the concept of nonresistance to evil, a basic element in the teaching of Leo Tolstoy. After months of arguing about these ideas, the sister and brother settle into a strained relationship of silence until she leaves to do vaccination work in the provinces. They part as strangers. At the close of the story, we learn the brother has died and is forgotten, and the narrator never saw the sister again. During this period of Chekhov's life, he was working through in his fiction his own response to Tolstoy's teaching, and this story, along with "The Beggar" and "An Encounter," reflects that process.[15]

Many of the stories from this period that portray a domestic setting revolve around the relationship between a husband and wife. In some of them, Chekhov continued to work within the traditional comic view of marriage promulgated by the entertainment magazines for which he had been writing. In "The Lottery Ticket" (Garnett) the satire is sharper than in most. Here a husband and wife in turn imaginatively explore the possibilities of winning a large amount of money from a lottery ticket. These imaginations reveal their limitations: both end up looking at each other with "hatred and anger," the husband knowing full well his wife did not include him in her fantasy and vice versa.

In a more accomplished story of marital tensions, "An Upheaval" (Garnett), Chekhov shifts the central consciousness to the central character of a young household governess, and the tensions between a husband and wife are explored indirectly through her. The governess is insulted because the wife has searched her room for a missing brooch. In the governess' recognition of the powerlessness of her situation, Chekhov also portrays the dynamics of the master-servant relationship. In the closing scene, when the governess is packing to leave because of the search, the husband comes to apologize and beg her to stay. The husband admits he took the brooch because his wife's tyrannical management of the household will not allow him access to his rightful property. But the governess cannot be persuaded to stay. In the husband's hesitant explanation of the truth of his marital relationship, the disabling nature of their domestic arrangement is rendered in a powerful manner.

The male counterpoint of the tyrannical wife in "An Upheaval" is the small-minded husband in "The Husband" (Garnett). At a club dance, the husband becomes indignant because his wife is having a good time, and his "petty feelings . . . swarmed in his heart like mice" (III, 297). To vent them, he forces his wife to go home early with him. She feels "miserable, insulted, and choking with hate" (III, 300), but like the husband in "An Upheaval," she is locked into this relationship through marriage and can do nothing.

Unhappiness in married life is also a key motivating force in the protagonist of "Drunk" (Garnett). This portrait of a wealthy merchant is among Chekhov's most psychologically complex from this period. The character is developed over the course of an evening when he becomes drunk at a restaurant with his lawyer. Like many Chekhovian protagonists, he abuses his power over others: the merchant mercilessly insults the waiters, attempting to demean them. During the course of the evening, the merchant confesses to the lawyer he despises his wife of two years, although by his own admission she is "handsome, clever, quiet" (142) and gives him no reason for his hatred. When she is in the room with him, his "whole soul boils" (141), and he can scarcely restrain himself from being rude to her. He fears she married him for his money. In his hatred and fear, and in his abuse of others, he recalls those drunken Dostoevsky characters trapped by their own destructive inner forces.

Stories of Love

The love relationship between a husband and wife is the focus of a couple of stories from this period. These stories are more distinguished by their place in Chekhov's development of the subject than by their literary merit. In "A Pink Stocking" (Garnett) and "Love" (Garnett) Chekhov's portrayal of the generic young men offers insight into the conventional gender attitudes toward marriage roles of the day. One young man thinks learned women are tedious, that they are "exacting, strict, and unyielding" (XIII, 289). But his wife never "pokes her nose into anything, does not understand so much, and never obtrudes her criticism"; in contrast to a bluestocking, she is a "pink stocking," a woman whose vocation is "to love her husband, to bear children and to mix salad" (289). In conclusion, the husband is satisfied with his wife, and is reconciled to what he views as her limitations.

While these early stories portray the lovers' initial happiness and then the married state of acceptance, Chekhov reverses this pattern in later stories such as "The Russian Master." In that story, the initial happiness of the protagonist is essentially the same, albeit portrayed with greater artistic skill, but his eventual married life becomes unacceptable as he grows to despise his domestic life and his spouse. This theme of unfulfillment develops from what D. S. Mirsky sees as the core of most of Chekhov's stories: the "mutual unsurpassable isolation of human beings and the impossibility of understanding each other."[16] This sense of isolation is the flip side of the coin of individuality, one of Chekhov's major concerns. It is another factor that contributes to the modern flavor of his work.

A variant on this theme occurs when the love is rejected, and instead of the person moving into a domestic situation, he or she remains alone and isolated. A couple of Chekhov's most accomplished stories from this period follow this pattern. In "Verotchka" (Garnett), Ognev, a census taker, walks through the August moonlight with Verotchka. Ognev relates that although he is twenty-nine, he has never had a romance, and his observation prompts Vera to confess hesitantly she loves him. But instead of responding in a positive manner to her, Ognev feels first confusion, then terror, then an acute and unpleasant awkwardness that leads to an inward revulsion. Ognev senses that this present experience with Vera is more important than "any statistics and books and truth" (VIII, 29); however, he finally tells her he does not love her. As he walks her back to her house, he realizes there is "so much life poetry and meaning" in her love it would "move a stone." Although he knows he is stupid not to respond to her, he is incapable of doing so. For the first time in his life, Ognev is learning "how little that a man does depends on his own will" (VIII, 31), a thought that will increasingly occur to Chekhov's protagonists. After his experience with Vera, Ognev knows he has lost "something very precious, something very near and dear which he would never find again" (VIII, 31), and he analyzes his "strange coldness." He decides it is not an intellectual coldness, but "simply impotence of soul, incapacity for being moved by beauty" (VIII, 32), brought on by his education and his lonely, nomadic lifestyle. This "impotence of soul" is an early example of a major concern of Chekhov: the inability of a person to overcome his isolation.

Within the year, Chekhov was to publish another story in which a man turns away from an experience that holds out promise of emotional fulfillment. The events in "The Kiss" (Garnett) revolve around the emotions of an ordinary man, a "little man," the quintessential Chekhovian hero. Ryabovitch, an artillery officer of common feelings and intelligence, is physically small in stature with sloping shoulders, spectacles, and lynxlike whiskers; his appearance suggests he is the "most undistinguished officer in the whole brigade" (IV, 178). One evening at a party, Ryabovitch accidentally wanders into a dark room where an unknown woman clasps him in her arms and passionately kisses him. When the woman realizes he is not the man with whom she had an appointed rendezvous, she flees, her face unseen, and Ryabovitch experiences a new sensation, wanting "to dance, to talk, to run into the garden, to laugh out loud" (IV, 184). He forgets his undistinguished appearance, and searches for the woman.

Although Ryabovitch cannot identify the woman, later at his quarters the thought of the kiss gives him an "intense groundless joy" (IV, 189). He feels something "extraordinary, foolish, but joyful and delightful" (IV, 191) has come into his life. When the brigade marches away to another district, he clings to this new agreeable thought to fight the boredom of his life. Ryabovitch considers himself an ordinary person, but now because of his dreams of a relationship with the woman, this ordinariness of his life "delighted him and gave him courage" (IV, 198). At summer's end, Ryabovitch is assigned back to the district where the party occurred. But as he passes the house where the party was held, he feels his dreams were all simply imaginings, and nothing will ever come of them. At this point, the whole world seems an "unintelligible, aimless jest"; his own life in particular "struck him as extraordinarily meager, poverty-stricken, and colorless" (IV, 205). Chekhov's artistic achievement in "The Kiss" lies first in making this common imagining of a "little man" so vividly convincing, so his mundane life swells with emotional richness; and second, in illustrating the humanness in his terrible disappointment when he achieves "true" perspective on his dreams. Ironically, the imagined experience leaves the "little man" finally poorer in spirit.

Stories of Adultery

Chekhov's interests in love and in domestic life amiss met at a fertile crossroad in the subject of adultery. Chekhov does not condemn the sexual activity of his characters; rather, the moral, or immoral, aspects of their sexual activity are defined by the attitudes and the actions of the characters themselves. In contrast to the humorous stories of adultery discussed above, published for the most part early in this period, these serious stories begin to appear in the spring of 1886. In many ways "The Chemist's Wife" (Garnett) is a transitional story. One newly serious element of Chekhov's is the wife's initial feeling of boredom and her resulting depression, which comes on her late one night as her husband, the pharmacist, sleeps. A doctor and an army officer come by the shop to flirt with her, and after the two men depart, she returns to her bedroom, from which she watches them whispering out in the street. Her heart beats violently "as though those two whispering outside were deciding her fate" (II, 322). When the officer returns and rings the shop bell, however, the husband wakes and waits on him. The story's humor develops as the officer, confronted by the husband's question of what he wants, replies, "Peppermint lozenges." This comic reversal echoes an earlier humorous description of the husband, when a greedy fly bites him as he happily dreams everyone in town has a cough and is buying cough drops from him. But these moments typical of Chekhov's humorous genre stories, are here subordinated to the serious tone. In the final scene, the wife watches from her bedroom window as the officer walks away down the street. Melting into tears, she realizes how unhappy she is and how no one is aware of that unhappiness.

The comic reversal is also an aspect of a story published a couple of weeks later, "The Chorus Girl" (Garnett), where the humor is again subordinated to a serious tone. The protagonist is Pasha, a chorus girl pursued by a bourgeois husband. One morning, the man's wife unexpectedly calls. While the husband is hiding in another room, the wife demands Pasha's jewelry, which the wife believes her husband has given Pasha. Afraid the wife will humiliate her, Pasha surrenders all her valuable jewelry, presents from other admirers, not the husband. The wife leaves "without uttering a word, without even nodding her head" (VIII, 10); thus the bourgeois wife asserts her position over the chorus girl, unfairly taking what is not hers, in a bitterly ironic comic reversal. This irony is compounded as the husband emerges from the other room after his wife's departure and contemptuously pushes Pasha aside as he declares how pure his wife is. Pasha is left weeping, with nothing, regretting the loss of her jewelry. Donald Rayfield uses "The Chorus Girl" to illustrate Guy de Maupassant's influence on Chekhov's writing about sexual mores in society (VIII, 62). In its tight, sparse structure, "The Chorus Girl" does achieve the objectivity toward which Chekhov had been striving. In a letter six months after the story was published, Chekhov declared a writer should be "as objective as a chemist; he should liberate himself from everyday subjectivity" (Heim, 62).

In several important ways, "A Misfortune" (Garnett), published a month after "The Chorus Girl," is more indicative of Chekhov's new direction not only with the subject of adultery but also with his narrative form. No humor lightens this account of a woman's struggle against, and final surrender to, a lover—the "misfortune" of the title. In this story Chekhov establishes the tone, the narrative pattern, and the character type that characterize some of his most important work. The key element in this particular story is the protagonist's decision whether or not to yield to the lover, for that decision contains the conflict between the moral consciousness of the protagonist and her mental and physical desires.

For that conflict to be significant, the moral consciousness of the protagonist must be well developed, as it is in Sofya, a young married woman with a daughter. She is a typical Chekhovian heroine, sensitive and intelligent, and married to a man with a white collar position. The lover Ilyin is a lawyer, a friend of five years who has declared his love for Sofya a few weeks before the opening action. Throughout the story, Sofya struggles between the physical and mental pleasure she feels in her relationship with Ilyin on the one hand, and her feeling of humiliation at her own "cowardice" on the other, her own "shamelessness" as a "chaste and high principled woman" (IV, 314). As the situation intensifies, Sofya realizes only people in trouble can understand "how far from easy it is to be the master of one's feelings and thoughts" (IV, 316), a realization common among Chekhov's characters. She decides she will reject Ilyin, but that evening at her dinner party she is filled with a sense of power from the control she has over him. Sofya flirts and feels amused, particularly by the tiepin which Ilyin wears, a red snake with diamond eyes. This snake, a phallic symbol and a traditional symbol of evil, suggests her physical desire as well as her fear of danger. Vaguely, Sofya senses "something is going wrong with me," and her conscience whispers she is behaving "boldly, foolishly."

But after Ilyin leaves, Sofya feels an oppressive, overpowering desire like a "boa-constrictor"—once again, Chekhov employs the image of the snake—gripping her limbs and her soul, "growing stronger every second." Fighting it, Sofya accuses herself of being an "immoral witch" and confesses to her husband she loves another man. Since her husband does not believe her, he lectures her listlessly for ten minutes on infidelity, then goes to bed. In a last attempt, Sofya asks her husband to take a walk with her, but receiving no response, she leaves alone to seek out Ilyin. Although she feels "hot with shame," she is overpowered by a force "stronger than shame, reason or fear" (IV, 327). Chekhov vividly portrays Sofya's conflict between physical desire and her wifely conscience. The basic tension between the conscious and unconscious forces that drives the character is the dynamic center of the story. Since the essential action here and in so many other Chekhov stories is located in the minds of his protagonists, critics apply the term "psychological realism" to his work. The narrative pacing, the employment of the third-person limited point of view, and the unfolding of scenes and details in this story are elements typical of psychological realism.

In the month following the publication of "A Misfortune," Chekhov published another remarkable story of adultery, "A Trifle From Life" (Garnett). If "A Misfortune" looks forward to Chekhov's line of later development, then this story shows him at his strongest in the sparser, more objective, dramatically focused narrative. Here Chekhov's narrative strategy, similar to "An Upheaval," published earlier that year, is to view the action in part from the perspective of a character outside the immediate relationship. In choosing Alyosha, the son of the adulterous mother, Chekhov gains more than an outside observer: he illustrates the painful, forced involvement of the other family members in the situation, and thus places the adultery within a larger framework. The scenes unfold with a surprising force, recording childhood trust in the face of adult betrayal, and culminating in a loss of innocence, a common theme in Chekhov's stories of childhood.

A month after the publication of "A Trifle From Life," another powerful story of adultery, "Mire" (Garnett), appeared. The story concerns two cousins who are sexually attracted to Susanna Rothstein, a wealthy Jewish woman. She persuades first the cousin who is engaged and then the other, who is married, to accept sexual favors for her monetary debts. The difference between the bourgeois ideal of sexual behavior and actual sexual practices is a central aspect of the story, as it is in "The Chorus Girl." Commenting on contemporary charges of anti-Semitism "Mire" occasioned, Karlinsky states it is only one of Chekhov's stories that examines "the reaction of sensitive Jews to the discrimination and repression under which they had to live"; Karlinsky believes Susanna's behavior is her "only way of asserting her own worth and of defying the hostility of the neighboring Russian noblemen" (Heim, 55).

Another sexually aggressive woman is Raissa, the sexton's wife in "The Witch" (Garnett). The couple lives in an isolated area three miles from the village, in a hut attached to a small church. The action occurs one evening when a mailman appears at the hut seeking shelter from a blizzard. Since young men have sought shelter in their hut during previous storms—hunters on a couple of occasions, a district clerk on another—the husband imagines Raissa supernaturally draws men to her. Raissa reminds him that before her father died, people regularly sought shelter in the hut during storms because of its location, and the husband is partially persuaded by her argument. But during the course of the evening, Raissa's eyes glow with a "strange fire" as she stares at the mailman, and when her husband steps outside, Raissa and the mailman embrace. Her husband glimpses them together on re-entering the hut, and when the mailman decides he must leave, the husband is very pleased. The "savage anger" Raissa exhibits after the mailman's departure—the result of her sexual frustration—convinces the husband she does indeed possess a mysterious, supernatural power, and he calls her a witch, believing she consorts with the devil. Although that conviction grieves him, it also gives Raissa a "peculiar, incomprehensible charm" for him, a poetic glamor (VI, 20). In drawing the parallel between the violent storm and Raissa's raging sexual frustration, Chekhov suggests a larger-than-life dimension to Raissa, an element more characteristic of the romantic tale than the realistic short story; however, since that view of the character is rooted in her husband's superstitions, the story does retain its realistic framework.

After 1887, Chekhov continued to explore the subject of adultery in his major work, both in such fiction as "The Party," "The Duel," "Three Years," and "A Lady With a Dog," and in his drama. Chekhov examined the rich subject from every angle: the betrayer and the betrayed, the husbands, the wives, the lovers, the other family members, both children and in-laws. Given Chekhov's concerns, it was a natural avenue for his development as a writer. Previous Russian writers such as Ivan Turgenev and Leo Tolstoy had treated the subject; Chekhov's contribution was linking the boredom, the grind of daily life, to the desire for sexual activity outside of marriage.

Stories of Peasants and Servants

Although Chekhov had written continuously about peasants since his early published stories such as "Because of Little Apples," during the period from 1885 to 1887 he began to portray this culture more seriously and with more commitment. The educated people of the day viewed the peasant idealistically, in part encouraged by the teachings of Leo Tolstoy. But Chekhov from the beginning was without illusions about the complex, human nature of the peasant. Commenting on his views, Chekhov wrote, "Peasant blood flows through my veins, and you can't astonish me with peasant virtues" (Heim, 261). His peasants are as much a mixture of virtue and vice, of type and individual as his bourgeois characters: kind-hearted, cruel, petty, compassionate, they crowd the pages of his work, fully reflecting the human landscape of Chekhov's day.

The influence of Turgenev's *The Sportsman's Sketches* (1852) is obvious in "The Huntsman" and "Agafya." As in Turgenev's "The Tryst" (1850), one of the stories in this collection, the relationship between the hard-working, long-suffering peasant woman and the footloose, gentry-favored peasant man is the focus of the action in "The Huntsman" (Garnett). A model of objective simplicity, the story is constructed around one scene composed of dialogue and highly selective character and landscape details. A key element is the setting: the forest, the time of year, and the specific weather all contribute to the scene's intensity. One summer afternoon, Yegor, a peasant out hunting, comes across his estranged wife, Pelagea, working with the village women. Pelagea still adores him and, "simply radiant with happiness," sits down to talk. She learns Yegor now spends all his time hunting and is living at the estate, where the landowner keeps Yegor as a sportsman for his amusement. Pelagea protests such hunting is not "proper work"; she views the physical labor of the village peasant as a cornerstone of domestic existence. But Yegor replies all he is good for is hunting. By hunting he lives differently than the ordinary peasant; in his own mind his experience of freedom has set him apart from the villagers. He states once "the spirit of freedom has taken a man you will never root it out of him" (VI, 244).

In this scene between Yegor and Pelagea, Chekhov follows his own advice that an author must keep his "hands and feet"—his subjective feelings—out of the story in the form of direct comment,[17] and must limit the natural description to its direct "character of relevance" (Yarmolinsky, 37). In this story, every natural detail becomes evocative, such as the ducks that fly overhead during the conversation: Yegor follows their flight with his eyes until they sink out of sight far beyond the forest, and at the close of the story, Yegor himself will walk away in that same direction, as mobile and as free as those very ducks. Chekhov believed that a writer must depict what the characters feel and think largely through action and dialogue (Yarmolinsky, 37). Singling out this story for comment on Chekhov's talent, Grigorovich displayed uncommon critical insight: Chekhov wrote more ambitious stories with wider concerns, but "The Huntsman" has that resonance which perfection generates.

Another outstanding story revolving around the relationship between a peasant man and woman is "Agafya" (Garnett), again a highly focused story with the action occurring during one evening and early the next morning. The events are narrated by a sportsman, a strikingly similar strategy to Turgenev's "The Tryst." The pace is more leisurely than in "The Huntsman," with more detailed descriptions of both the characters—Savka and Agafya—and nature. Like the peasant in "The Huntsman," Savka is free from common peasant life: he is a man who feels no inclination for physical labor. Like an animal, Savka is attuned to his physical surroundings, and he has a face as "open, soft, and expressive as a woman's" (VI, 120). Since Savka will not discipline himself to work, he has been made the watchman for the village garden. He and the narrator discuss various topics, among them the summer night sounds, until Agafya appears for a tryst with Savka.

Agafya has been married for only a year, but she eagerly meets Savka for this sexual rendezvous. She drinks vodka with him until she knows she should go home or be discovered by her husband. But some "invincible and implacable force" (VI, 129) seems to keep her with Savka. Like the force that grips the bourgeois Sofya in "A Misfortune" and the men in "Mire," Agafya is in the grip of sexual desire. When she finally does leave, it is morning. Her husband waits as she fearfully crosses the fields toward him and the village, the symbol of the community values. Savka tells the narrator now he will be flogged again by the village court like before, for he has had numerous affairs with the village women, who voluntarily bring him food and clothes.

In this narrative of simple people, the scene with Agafya returning to her husband to receive a beating is an indictment of the village mores. In a letter Chekhov declared he hated violence in all its forms (Heim, 109). Elsewhere Chekhov's indictment of the brutality in peasant lives is even more damning, such as in "Peasants" and "In the Hollow." But nowhere does Chekhov combine his indictment with such attractive, energetic characters as Savka and Agafya.

Since Chekhov's characters are realistically grounded in their society, his work rewards a sociological critique. One critic declared that if all the other literature of Chekhov's generation were to disappear, "a sociologist could paint a picture on the broad canvas of life of the 'eighties and 'nineties and its background with his writings alone."[18] In his humorous stories of peasant life, Chekhov views character as an integral part of the larger social environment, the peasant community. These stories are basically similar to "Sergeant Prishibeyev" in narrative technique, tone, and length. Both "The Village Elder—A Little Scene" and "Women Make Trouble—A Little Scene" are typical of Chekhov's earlier comic approach and narrative form. As suggested by the subtitles—"A Little Scene"—the emphasis is on dialogue, with only a few selected details on the settings and the actions of the characters. These stories could be converted easily into plays with stage directions, and in fact, in referring to similarly constructed stories, A. P. Chudakov uses a term that translates as "prose play."[19] Both stories, like "Sergeant Prishibeyev," depict the judicial system. In "The Village Elder" (Yarmolinsky 1954), a lawyer tells of a hard-working, successful peasant who is taken advantage of by the members of his village. In "Women Make Trouble" (Yarmolinsky 1954), an examining magistrate investigates a case in which a peasant has beaten his wife. One of the peasant witnesses gives testimony; his dialogue comprises the core of the story.

Chekhov's most effective story in this vein is "A Malefactor" (Garnett). A magistrate questions a peasant about removing nuts from the railroad bed, and the peasant explains he uses the nuts as weights for fishing. The magistrate declares the nuts are needed to hold the rails in place to prevent railway accidents, but the peasant believes that, since the railroad has thousands and thousands of such nuts, it should not miss the few he uses. The magistrate, however, sentences the peasant to prison, and the story closes with the peasant bitterly protesting he has not been judged fairly. As in the other two stories, one of Chekhov's concerns is the difficulty of rendering justice; he allows the nature of the culprit and the crime to bring into question the fairness of the sentence.

In contrast to these peasant stories is a group of stories in the naturalistic mode, such as "At the Mill" (Yarmolinsky 1947), with its mean-spirited, brutal miller, and "Darkness" (Garnett), in which the brother of a peasant sentenced to prison pleads for his release. But the naturalism of these stories is transformed in "An Encounter" (Yarmolinsky 1947). In the peasant Kuzma, Chekhov creates one of his more complex characters, a sociologically maladjusted individual who like the protagonist in "Drunk" recalls the psychologically self-tortured characters of Dostoevsky. Kuzma, regularly flogged by the village court, has been in and out of prison all his life for stealing and fighting. In this story, he not only steals church money from an itinerant lay peasant named Yefrem, but also confronts Yefrem about the theft. Yefrem's response is that he himself will not seek retribution, but Kuzma must answer to God for it. The dramatic tension of the story arises from the danger Yefrem is in: Kuzma is fully capable of physical violence, and the threat of assault, even murder, is in the air. The response of Yefrem again recalls certain Dostoevsky characters—in this instance, a character such as Alyosha in *The Brothers Karamozov* (1880), who embodies Christian virtues. Yefrem also represents the ideal of nonresistance as preached by Leo Tolstoy; Chekhov's exploration of that concept in this story is resolved as Kuzma returns what money he has left to Yefrem, abating the threat of violence. The naturalistic determinism of the story—in which social and environmental forces overcome an individual so he cannot exercise free will—is thus mitigated by the actions of Yefrem.

A few months after "An Encounter," one of Chekhov's favorite stories, "Happiness" (Garnett), appeared. In "Happiness" he also explores abstract concepts through concrete peasant characters, and in so doing, again transforms the naturalistic mode. On the vast reaches of the steppe, two shepherds discuss various topics with an estate overseer. In this landscape of great emptiness and broad sky, human events seemed dwarfed by nature. Even the sheep have "tedious and oppressive" thoughts, their days and nights "crushing them into apathy" (VI, 252). (The marvelous detail of this landscape anticipates that of a novella Chekhov wrote the following year, "The Steppe.") One of the shepherds, a toothless old man, describes his relationship with another old peasant who died that spring. The dead peasant had lived in solitude, doing old women's jobs his whole life, behavior the old shepherd superstitiously believes was a sign he had consorted with the devil. The shepherd claims the devil whistled through the peasant's melons in his garden, and one time the devil assumed the shape of a laughing pike that the peasant caught. The overseer, although a "serious, reasonable man" (VI, 251), concurs that such supernatural events are indeed possible, implicitly suggesting he shares this view of the world. The shepherd recalls that when the peasant was flogged for his inappropriate behavior, he cursed the people of the village with typhus. The peasant would have been killed for that, but the old people of the village were convinced he knew where a treasure was hidden.

The subject of treasure, once introduced, becomes the general topic as the overseer tells tales of gold buried in the surrounding hills, and, in an analogy, equates treasure with human happiness: like buried treasure, happiness can be always near, but unattainable, so that one dies without possessing it. This attitude toward happiness becomes a recurring motif in several of Chekhov's subsequent works, in which characters believe that happiness is presently denied people, but that future generations will achieve it. The next morning after the overseer departs, the young shepherd ponders on the "fantastic fairy-tale character of human happiness" (261). Such thoughts occur on the boundless steppe where there is a feeling of "endless time and utter indifference to man." (261). But in the very imaginings of these men, the limitations of that environment have been transcended, so the story is finally an affirmation, eschewing the defeat of the human will typical of works of naturalism.

In analyzing the "unique fascination" that emanates from such Chekhov stories as "Happiness" and the spell that fascination exercises on the reader, Charles Trimmer sees the key ingredient as the elements of "hope and expectation" blended masterfully with the elements of "helplessness and despair."[20] That blending is superbly realized in "Dreams" (Garnett), in which two peasant constables are escorting a tramp on foot to see an examining magistrate. In narrative structure, this story resembles "The Huntsman" with its one continuous scene. Also as in "The Huntsman," details of the setting, such as the fog through which the men walk, become significant. As they walk, the tramp tells his stories: his mother was a house serf who bore him illegitimately, and he believes he is the son of the master. Since the tramp is a frail little man with a poor constitution, the constables allow him to rest, and during this break, the tramp adds that he is an escaped convict. His mother was convicted of poisoning the master because he had taken another mistress; since the tramp handed the glass to the master, he was convicted as an accomplice. The tramp refuses to give his name because he hopes to escape detection and simply be exiled to Siberia where he can begin a new life.

The tramp's lyrical description of Siberia suggests the "dreams" of the title. Even the dull constables respond to the tramp's imaginings, which center around the life of a free man in nature. This man is pictured fishing and hunting—"strong in body and bold in spirit"—a man without fear of society or fear of his own solitude. (This portrait of life in Siberia resembles a common idealistic perception of life in the American West.) In the tramp's imaginings, he transcends the impenetrable wall of fog that lies like a "weight on the heart" and stands "like a prison wall before the eyes" (VI, 95). The constables, in response, call up a picture of man's freedom and liberty "such as they had never seen" (VI, 95). But then one of the constables reminds the tramp that in his ill health, he could never survive the trip to Siberia. As the three of them resume walking, hopelessness and despair settle over the tramp so that he is more bent over than ever.

A similar blending of affirmation and despair characterizes one of Chekhov's masterpieces from this period, "Misery" (Garnett). As in "Dreams" and "The Huntsman," the events are highly focused in time, occurring one evening as Iona, a cabman, drives fares around St. Petersburg. Earlier in the week, the cabman's son, also a cabby, died in the hospital, and the despair Iona now feels is reflected in the setting, an evening twilight of continuously falling wet snow. During the course of the evening, Iona secures only a few fares, and with each, he attempts to tell his passengers of his grief, and thus alleviate it. But these passengers are strangers with no time for him. Unlike the peasants in the village from which Iona came with his horse, no one among the thousands who surround him will listen. Iona's loneliness grows as the evening progresses until his "misery was immense, beyond all bounds" (IX, 62). Although no one can see it, if "Iona's heart was to burst and his misery flow out, it would flood the whole world, it seems" (IX, 62). Iona returns early to the yard, where once again he attempts to relate his grief to a young cabman who, not listening, falls asleep. With no one available to listen, Iona feeds his horse, a mare. Since no person will share his misery, Iona begins to speak to her, pouring out his heartache, and she "munches, listens, and breathes on her master's hands." Ironically, the cabby thus finds relief from his despair not in his fellow man, but in this fellow creature.

Another story with an ironic dimension is "Anyuta" (Garnett), in which a student is taking advantage of a young servant woman. Anyuta is a poor seamstress in her middle twenties who has lived with half a dozen students in as many years, serving as their sexual partner as well as their servant until they graduate and move on, forgetting her. During a winter afternoon, the medical student with whom she lives is preparing for an examination, so he has Anyuta disrobe in the cold room and traces her ribs with a black marker to solve his anatomy question. When a young artist drops by and requests that Anyuta serve as a model for a painting of Psyche, the medical student orders her to comply, and during her absence decides he should part from her. But Anyuta weeps when he tells her, so he relents, agreeing that she can stay another week. In a fine analysis of the mythological aspects of the story, which center in the Psyche figure, Renota Poggioli concludes that with "unobtrusive, but penetrating irony, Chekhov makes Anyuta's body serve the higher purposes of art and science."[21] The irony arises from the contrast between the attitude of the two men who consider Anyuta their inferior, while actually in her selfless behavior she is their moral superior. "Anyuta" resembles "The Chorus Girl," calling into question the values of the bourgeois.

Stories of Children

One of Chekhov's favorite subjects during this period was children, who appear in many of the stories discussed above, including "Oysters," "The Privy Councillor," "A Trifle From Life," and "Home." These stories were written with an adult audience in mind, but Chekhov also wrote stories for children during this period, such as "Kashtanka—A Story" (Garnett), a tale with a lost dog for a protagonist that appeared in illustrated editions for children. His 1889 collection *Children (Detvora)* contained stories about children. But after "The Steppe," published in 1888, Chekhov largely turned away from the subject with the notable exception of "Patch" (Hingely), an 1895 story about a she-wolf. Many of Chekhov's stories about children appeal to both younger and older readers, in a manner similar to that of Charles Dickens's "A Christmas Carol" (1843) and Mark Twain's *Huckleberry Finn* (1884).

Two of Chekhov's most critically discussed stories with child protagonists are "Vanka" (1886) and "Sleepy" (written in 1887; published in 1888). Both are about a peasant child sent to the city as a servant, and who lives a life of hardship. The humor in "Vanka" (Garnett) is predicated upon the situation of the peasant in the big city, a Russian genre that resembles the "city boy, country boy" stories and jokes common in the United States. Nine-year-old Vanka writes his grandfather a Christmas letter in which he details his hardships as a shoemaker's apprentice and begs his grandfather to send for him. But in mailing the letter, Vanka simply addresses it to "Grandfather in the Village" so that it is undeliverable. This ending is reminiscent of Chekhov's earlier period.

Chekhov transcends the comic mode, however, in presenting a portrait of a suffering child as he did in "Oysters." Vanka's parents are dead: his mother was a house serf, and on her death, Vanka was apprenticed. His master physically abuses Vanka, and gives him little to eat, porridge and a few pieces of bread a day. When the master's baby cries, Vanka must rock it to sleep—the central situation in "Sleepy." If Vanka falls asleep tending the child, he is beaten. He concludes his letter declaring his life is "wretched, worse than any dog's" (XII, 94). Interspersed with these complaints are Vanka's memories of village life, with lyrical passages describing a clear winter night on which "the Milky Way is as distinct as though it had been washed and rubbed with snow" (XII, 91). But now Vanka, the orphan in the city, is as lonely as Iona, the cabman in "Misery," and his heart is filled with anguish. Once again blending hope and despair, Chekhov's artistic achievement is in creating the reality of this nine-year-old with such compelling intensity.

A child's reality also is vividly realized in "Sleepy" (Garnett). But it is the distorted reality—similar in ways to that of "Typhus"—of a thirteen-year-old servant girl, Varka, who is emotionally and physically exhausted. Throughout the story, because of sleep deprivation, Varka's world becomes increasingly irrational. She is so driven by the demands of her master she finally becomes completely irrational and strangles the baby she is tending simply so she may sleep. The tone here is more somber, and the mood more hopeless, than in "Vanka." Like Vanka, Varka is a village peasant in the world of the city. She dreams of home, but her dreams are not the pleasant imaginings of Vanka: instead, they are bleak images, one of her father dying in a pain so terrible he could not utter a single word. These dreams blend with smooth transitions into her waking hallucinations, so that in the view of Gleb Struve, the story is "a model of terseness," of Chekhov's famous brevity rendered with "the most effective artistic means."[22] Struve believes there is much to be said for preferring certain stories from this period, such as "Sleepy," which display Chekhov's "exquisite mastery," to longer, later stories such as "A Dreary Story," "The Duel," or "Ward Number Six" (476).[23]

Other stories in which Chekhov portrays peasant children are "A Day in the Country" (Garnett), in which a pair of orphans receive help from an old cobbler, and "The Runaway" (Garnett), where the child's fictional reality recalls "Vanka," but is darker in tone. In stories about children of other classes, Chekhov depicts the same childhood reality with one important difference: these stories are without the compelling urgency and the desperation in the characters common to the peasant stories. In "Grisha" (Garnett), a delightful story, Chekhov achieves the remarkable effect of presenting the reality of a two-and-one-half-year-old child—an artistic accomplishment roughly equal to portraying the feverish mind in "Typhus" or the wolf's mind in "Patch." The events are structured around an outing Grisha experiences with his nurse.

A companion piece to "Grisha" is "A Cook's Wedding" (Garnett). Chubby little Grisha, now seven, is once again the protagonist, and once again the story is structured around learning experiences that leave him emotionally upset. But the experiences of this older child are more complex, more subtle. The house cook is to be married to a cabman, with the nurse serving as matchmaker. Grisha is confronted with the complex situation of courtship and marriage, and with the correspondingly baffling behavior of the participants. At the close of the story when the newly married cabman demands an advance on the cook's wages, Grisha is exposed to the concept of property rights in marriage, and he concludes there is a great injustice in them. Through the eyes of this innocent child, Chekhov explores larger social issues from a different perspective.

In other stories Chekhov portrays the world of peer relationships among children. In "Children" (Garnett), nine-year-old Grisha plays cards with his brothers and sisters and the cook's son in a delightful scene, capturing the special bond children have with siblings and other children their age. And in "Boys" (Garnett), the imaginative doings of a pair of preadolescents attempting to run away to America resemble some of the antics of Twain's Tom Sawyer. Chekhov's most complex story with a child protagonist is in the novella, "The Steppe," which will be discussed later.

Stories of the Elderly

Chekhov portrays elderly characters throughout this period, such as the old shepherd peasant in "Happiness" and the benevolent old cobbler in "A Day in the Country." But in some stories, he focuses on the special situations, problems, and attitudes of the elderly. Early in this period, Chekhov's stories were undergoing the transition from humorous to serious, and "Old Age" (Garnett), published in 1885, illustrates that transition. It resembles his "prose play" stories in that it largely consists of the dialogue between two characters. The typical Chekhovian comic reversal occurs as an old man learns that, in his underhanded designs to escape his first marriage, he has engaged an attorney who, in turn, took advantage of him. The story closes with the old man in despair from the pain he caused his first wife.

Two weeks after "Old Age" was published, "Sorrow" (Garnett) appeared, a more accomplished story that also exhibits transitional elements from the humorous to the serious. But in contrast to "Old Age," with its focus on dialogue, this story is structured largely around an elderly man's thoughts as he drives his sick wife to the doctor in a snowstorm. The old man, a peasant craftsman, a turner, mutters his thoughts to himself, sometimes addressing the imaginary doctor at the hospital ahead, sometimes addressing his wife, promising he will never beat her again. This comic monologue is typical of Chekhov's early period. But when the turner realizes that his wife has died en route, the tone darkens. In an epiphany, the turner realizes he has lived the past forty years with his wife as if in a fog, his drunkenness and quarreling allowing for no true feeling. He has wasted his life, one of the harshest self-evaluations an elderly person can make. The images of the swirling snow and of his wife's dead body knocking about in the sleigh behind him metaphorically mirror the turner's thoughts, so Beverly Hahn sees the story as essentially poetic, a kind of poem in prose form, the images functioning as a "composite metaphor for human states and feelings."[24]

The close of the story finds the turner at the hospital, where he has awakened after losing consciousness in the storm. In a final irony, the doctor tells him he will lose his arms and legs from frostbite, thus destroying his livelihood as a turner. Like "Sleepy," the story closes on a hopeless note. The Russian critic Vladimir Yermilov views the blending of the comic and serious elements in "Sorrow" as mutually dependent; never before in literature, Yermilov claims, had there been anything like this wealth of philosophical, psychological, and artistic content in a "miniature tale" (90–91). The central premise in "Sorrow" of an elderly man evaluating his past with his wife and finding himself deficient in their relationship looks forward to a longer story, "Rothschild's Fiddle," a masterpiece published almost a decade later in 1894.

The despair resulting from poverty, often linked to the elderly, finds its most powerful statement in "The Dependents" (Garnett). An old artisan has exhausted his resources and has no money to buy food for his dog and horse, his "dependents." Drunk on vodka, he takes his animals to the slaughterhouse where he witnesses their deaths by blows to their heads. After viewing their corpses, in his "drunken foolishness" he goes up to the stand and puts forward his own head, "ready for a blow" (XII, 223). In its naturalistic fashion, the pathetic despair of the old man overwhelms any sense of hope and expectation in the story. In his foolishness the man's drunken action ends in pathos, again a typical Chekhovian twist that functions as closure to the story.

Chekhov uses an elderly protagonist to explore the relationship of the present to the past in "The Pipe" (Garnett). An old shepherd contrasts the world of the past, with its plentiful, natural environment, to the world of the present, polluted and corrupted by mankind. The events of the story, which revolve around a conversation between an old peasant shepherd and an overseer, resemble "Happiness," published a few months earlier. The story opens during a rainy afternoon when the overseer is hunting and comes across the old shepherd herding a band of horses, cows, and sheep. Their conversation turns to the lack of game, and the old man declares all nature—the animals, the forests and rivers, even humankind—is declining and perishing. The reason for this situation, the old shepherd states, is that man has turned away from God. In his religious belief, the old shepherd embodies a premodern conception of the world common among the peasants. This view of the world maintains that all the elements of the universe—"the sun, and the sky, and the forest, and the rivers, and the creatures"—must exist in their proper relationships with each other: "Each has been put to its appointed task and knows its place" (VI, 105). In the old shepherd's view, that ordered world is disintegrating, and he mourns its passing. In exploring this change in the natural world—the disappearance of certain animals and the ecological system that supports them—Chekhov was far ahead of his time. Although Chekhov's views on conservation are most widely known through the character Astrov in *Uncle Vanya*, those ideas were explored previously in "The Pipe."

Stories of Religion

Although Chekhov declared he was not a believer in the traditional sense, he respected organized religion, and in a couple of his best stories from this period, he portrayed characters with a deep commitment to traditional religious life.[25] Chekhov obviously admires these characters. Among the most sympathetic is Father Yakov Smirnov, the young village priest in "A Nightmare" (Garnett). Donald Rayfield notes Chekhov is not often viewed as a writer whose work stirred people to action, but the vision of poverty and degradation portrayed in "A Nightmare" did generate a reaction in readers that amazed Chekhov (55). The priest is viewed through the eyes of a young member of the district board, Kunin, a landowner disappointed in the priest's shabby look and preoccupied manner. Not until the end of the story when the priest appeals to Kunin for a secretary's position does he learn the priest's true situation: the priest is living in extreme poverty with his wife, actually going hungry so he may fulfill the religious obligations of his village. The realization completely changes Kunin's attitude toward the priest, and he becomes sympathetic to his needs. This movement of the central consciousness from innocence to experience is a classic structure for the short story. Ernest Simmons believes "A Nightmare" is one of the half-dozen best stories Chekhov wrote during this period (132). It reflects Chekhov's great compassion for the "little man" who struggles to live a life of integrity. Frank O'Connor, who had a high opinion of Chekhov's work, termed this story Chekhov's "most savage indictment" of Russia's treatment of its intelligentsia.[26]

A story published two weeks after "A Nightmare" is one of Chekhov's most widely translated masterpieces, "Easter Eve" (Garnett). When Donald Rayfield terms "Easter Eve" the most "magical" of Chekhov's stories of 1886, he refers to the wonderful power and the complexity of tone that the details of the setting and the characters generate. The religious character is again viewed from the outside by a secular narrator. This anonymous narrator, who functions as Chekhov's own persona, is visiting a monastery on Easter Eve for the mass celebration and festivities. In crossing a flood-swollen river to the monastery grounds, he engages in conversation with the ferryman, a lay brother named Ieronim. Earlier that day, a monk named Nikolay died, and the ferryman is filled with grief. Unlike the cabman in "Misery," this ferryman can unburden himself to a sympathetic ear. He recalls that his friend Nikolay was a composer of canticles. The ferryman's lengthy description of Nikolay's canticles actually constitutes a guide to the aesthetic appreciation of the form, in which every line must possess "softness, graciousness and tenderness; not one word should be hard or rough or unsuitable" (VII, 55).[27] After the journey across the river, the narrator participates in the church services throughout the night, during which he realizes how truly sensitive and religious the simple ferryman is. Through this narrator, as through the consciousness of the young landowner in "A Nightmare," the moral nature of the religious hero—in this instance, the ferryman—is revealed.

Early the next morning, after the services and the festivities have concluded, the narrator recrosses the river, and the ferryman is still at his post, transporting two dozen monastery visitors back across the watery expanse. The ferryman's physical labor is analogous to his spiritual presence, which brings the narrator to a recognition of man's love for his fellow man—the true religious feeling of Easter. It was not in the church service itself with its "childish irresponsible joy" and "senseless jostling and shoving" that the real spirit of Easter resides, but in the simple faith of that ferryman. Ironically, the ferryman could not attend the services that mean so much to him because of his duty to his fellow man.

In her fine analysis of "Easter Eve," Beverly Hahn develops the dimensions of Chekhov's vision of the world as a nineteenth-century humanist: she posits a basic tension between Chekhov's "idealism and optimism about human capabilities" on the one hand, and his "resigned realism about the conditions and restrictions on life as things are" on the other (VII, 71).

Both "A Nightmare" and "Easter Eve" appeared six weeks after "The Requiem" (Garnett), where the initial conflict is between the protagonist, a shopkeeper, and his priest. This earlier story retains elements of Chekhov's transition between the comic and the serious, with the opening portrait of the shopkeeper essentially that of a comic character. Chekhov describes his dress as that of a dandy, but with huge clumsy galoshes. The shopkeeper has requested a requiem (a mass for the dead) for his daughter. In his written request he has referred to his daughter as "the harlot Mariya" since she had become an actress after her move to the city. The priest is outraged at the word "harlot," and takes the shopkeeper to task, but when the shopkeeper says he understands his error, the priest orders the service to begin. With the requiem in progress, the dramatic focus shifts to the shopkeeper's memories of his daughter. At this point in the action, the tone becomes serious. Through these memories, the lack of communication—a major Chekhovian theme—between father and daughter becomes evident. Although the story does not possess the poetic intensity of "Easter Eve," the perfection of its simple form recalls "The Huntsman."

"The Letter" (Garnett) is set in the private chambers of a supervisory priest on Easter eve. The situation involves an interview between the supervisor and an old, poor priest with nine children. The old priest has been relieved of his official duties because of "intemperate" habits: in his desperate poverty, he has been celebrating unlawful marriages for money. Irony develops when this disreputable old priest is revealed as the only character who exhibits the true religious spirit of forgiveness.

As in "Easter Eve," the anonymous narrator in "Uprooted—An Incident of My Travels" (Garnett) is visiting a monastery. Because of their similar narrators and religious settings, the two stories can be viewed as companion pieces. In this story, the protagonist, a convert from Judaism, is the narrator's roommate in the hostel. The modern aspect of the character is rooted in his spiritual sufferings, which resemble the existential dread of Dostoevsky's heros. The narrator realizes that across Russia "a vast multitude of such uprooted creatures was pacing at that moment along highways and sidetracks" (VII, 150). But since the dramatic focus in "Uprooted" is not as sharp as that in "Easter Eve," the characters and events do not reverberate with the same level of intensity.

Another Easter story is "An Endless Process" (Smith), a comic "prose play." The humor arises from the dialogue between an old woman and a church sexton who has difficulties drawing up a list of names for prayers. Chekhov's transition from a comic genre writer to a serious literary artist is obvious in his sequence of stories on religion: from the early "An Endless Process," through "The Requiem," a transitional story with both serious and comic elements, to a completely somber story, "A Nightmare," to the masterpiece "Easter Eve." After this period Chekhov went on to write other stories on the subject of religion, including "The Student," one of his favorite stories, and "The Bishop," a late masterpiece.

Stories of Art

As a literary artist, Chekhov knew a great deal about the creative process, and a half-dozen stories from this period explore that subject. Among the best is "Art" (Garnett), about a peasant who creates a "jordan"—a religious setting on an ice-covered river for the blessing of the water on the feast of the Epiphany, the twelfth day of Christmas. The peasant Seryozhka is an unlikely artist, a "non-entity, a sluggard, a drunkard, a wastrel" (XII, 271). But when it comes to making the jordan, this peasant is transformed into an exacting perfectionist. The creative process works through him as he prepares the ice lectern and carves a dove from ice. Then, in great excitement, he races about the village "like one possessed" requesting painting materials. The villagers, like the members of a medieval community, feel his art is "not his personal affair but something that concerns them all, the whole people" (271). Despite the peasant's threats and swearing, the villagers freely provide him with emotional support and necessary materials, for they believe "one creates, the others help him." When he is creating, he is "at once something higher, a servant of God" (XII, 271). This story is not only a portrayal of the creative process, but also a picture of the peasant village functioning as a community. In contrast to this positive portrait of the artistic process is the portrayal of the painter Yegor Savvitch in "Talent" (Garnett). Yegor spends his time dreaming about being famous and entertaining his painter friends, but not actually painting.

Stories about writers include "Hush" (Garnett), a delightful story about a journalist, and "In Spring" (Dunnigan), about a secluded writer. The structure of "In Spring" with its essaylike rhetoric is atypical for Chekhov, although the satire and light tone recalls his early comic stories. Chekhov's most complex story about writers from this period is "A Story Without an End" (Garnett). The writer is the narrator of the story, and his ambitious subject, the nature of man in the world. The story is divided into two sections, with the first devoted to the writer's experience with an acquaintance who attempted suicide, and the second organized around an intellectual search for knowledge about life. Although one result of this intellectual search is the knowledge that one cannot retain an emotional experience with its full intensity for any length of time—for example, the attempted suicide of the first section—another result is the emotional regret about such loss. The resolution between these two kinds of knowledge provides closure to the story.

Stories of the Theater

During this period, Chekhov also wrote a half-dozen stories involving theatre. These, like the stories of religion, illustrate at first a continuation of the early genre pieces, and then a transformation to his new serious direction. In the mode of those early genre pieces is "A Play" (Garnett), in which a well-known writer grudgingly consents to listen to a woman read her play. But the play is so boring with its stereotypical characters and stock situations that the writer completely loses his patience and kills the woman with a paperweight. Although the comic situation in "A Theatre Manager Under the Sofa" (Hinchcliffe) does not employ such slapstick, the action does resemble burlesque entertainment: an actress discovers the theater manager hiding under her dressing room sofa while she is changing.

The theater stories that focus on character as opposed to comic action point further toward Chekhov's new serious direction. Most of these stories portray actors in their private lives, and although none of the stories is a masterpiece, they exhibit an integrity that reflects Chekhov's increasing artistic development and his interest in theater. In an early character study, "Mari d'Elle" (Garnett), an opera singer has made a success of herself through her own determination and must now deal with the schemes of her husband, who lives off her earnings. A more accomplished story is "The Jeune Premier" (Garnett) in which the provincial actor who plays the romantic lead—the "jeune premier"—ironically displays very unromantic behavior in real life when challenged to a duel.

Two other stories about actors lead to an early Chekhov one-act play. In "An Actor's End" (Garnett) an old actor who plays the good-hearted simpleton and the "heavy" father has a heart attack. Before he dies, he realizes that he has wasted his life in acting. This basic idea is more fully developed in "Calchas" (Miller), in which an old actor at the end of his career realizes he, too, has given up his life for acting, and the sacrifice in the end was not worthwhile. Chekhov recast this story as the one-act play *Swan Song* (1887), which, as Vera Gottlieb illustrates, explores theater as a metaphor for life (132).[28]

Chekhov went on to write about an actress a few years later in his 1889 work, "A Dreary Story," but after completing his first mature, full-length play, *Ivanov*, in the fall of 1887, Chekhov largely treated the subject of theater in the plays themselves, especially in *The Seagull*.

Stories of Various Subjects

A number of stories from this period do not fit easily into any broad category. The best contain superb character portrayals, such as in "The Schoolmaster" (Garnett), where Chekhov's objective approach is at its most effective in presenting a sick, irritable teacher. The man discovers he is terminally ill and his colleagues are being kind because they expect him to die in a short time, and the discovery fills his soul with "unutterable despair." This trim story without a wasted scene is perfect in terms of form. As a practicing physician, Chekhov did have a special insight into the manner in which illness effects people, and the description of this terminally ill school teacher is compelling in its accuracy. Throughout his career, Chekhov continued to occasionally treat the ill, particularly peasants, and was active in fighting epidemics.

Chekhov's medical background is also apparent in some other stories from this period with doctors as protagonists. The most widely known of these doctor figures is Kirilov in "Enemies" (Garnett). The doctor has just lost his only child, a six-year-old son, to diphtheria when a landowner requests the doctor accompany him to his wife's sick bed. In despair, the doctor refuses, but the landowner pleads so effectively that the doctor finally consents. At the landowner's estate, the two men discover the wife had faked her illness to enable her to run away with another man. In a moment of vulnerability, the landowner relates his feelings to the doctor, but, instead of sympathizing, the doctor becomes enraged, and the two men engage in a cruel argument that makes them enemies for life. The story is weakened by Chekhov's moralizing, a rare fault for him by this point in his artistic development. Rather than allow the events to speak for themselves, Chekhov tells the reader that Kirilov's thoughts about the landowner were "unjust and inhumanly cruel," and that Kirilov's negative convictions about people like the landowner are "unjust and unworthy of the human heart" (XI, 34). One strength of the story, however, is the figure of Dr. Kirilov, for although herolike, he possesses convincingly human limitations. Another strength lies in the details of the sick room in the opening scene, which are rendered with the vividness and the immediacy of a realistic painting.

In Chekhov's Christmas story for 1886, "On the Road" (Garnett), the protagonist Liharev is delayed by a snowstorm and stays at a rural inn on Christmas Eve with his young daughter. The personification of the storm's fury recalls "The Witch." Another traveller, a young woman from a local landowner's family, is also forced to lay over at the inn. She and the protagonist engage in a lengthy discussion of the various beliefs—such as the abolition of private property and the non-resistance to evil—for which he has worked. Liharev's wandering life and his restless spirit resemble the character of the religious convert in "Uprooted"; like that convert, Liharev is not at all pleased with his life. Although he has never intentionally lied or "done evil," he has been a "misfortune" to all who have loved him: to the members of his family, who are ashamed of him, and most of all, to his devoted wife, who died worn out from his "reckless activity." Liharev's present conviction is his belief in womankind. The possibility that Liharev will change his life in a significant manner, and that the young woman will change hers, lies heavy in the air. But at the close of the story, after the storm abates enough to travel, they part, each in a separate direction, each lonely and isolated. Like much of Chekhov's best fiction, the story ends with the protagonist's refusals, or incapacity, to take the opportunity to change his or her life.

The abstract ideology espoused by Liharev reappears in several stories that Chekhov wrote during this period, when he was most impressed with the thinking of Leo Tolstoy. Other stories in this group are "Excellent People"; "An Encounter"; and "The Beggar" (Garnett), in which a Petersburg lawyer gives an alcoholic beggar a job chopping wood. Eventually, the beggar becomes cured of his drinking habit, and through the lawyer's good graces, secures a respectable position. The lawyer takes great pride in this accomplishment until he learns that it was not his actions, but those of his cook, who actually chopped the wood for the beggar, that inspired him to change. In contrast to the characters in "On the Road," the characters in "The Beggar" are not sufficiently well-drawn to give depth to the narrative. "The Beggar," however, with its straightforward simplicity, is closer to the spirit of Tolstoy's thought than any other Chekhov story.

A more impressive example of Chekhov's craftsmanship is "A Trivial Incident" (Garnett). This story, like "Easter Eve" and "Uprooted," is narrated in a sensitive first-person by a character who functions as Chekhov's persona, and who is involved in the action. One subject of "A Trivial Incident" is the life and values of the aristocracy. The prince embodies aristocratic values: he has the manners of a retired army officer, he is straightforward and honest, and he is so far in debt that his estate is in jeopardy. He has no profession (another characteristic of the aristocracy) and will soon be forced to find a job in order to survive. A trivial incident dramatically presents the prince's character. The head clerk of the estate on which the prince and the narrator are hunting informs them that shooting in those woods is forbidden. When the prince learns that the owner of the estate is Princess Shabelsky, he requests that the narrator personally ask for permission to hunt. As the prince and the narrator drive to the manor house, the narrator presents the background events: had the prince been able to lie to the father of the princess, who desired that he marry his daughter, the prince would now be a millionaire. The prince's honesty is one his aristocratic values, which ironically are detrimental to him in his present situation.

When the men reach the manor house, the narrator enters alone and meets the princess. The narrator's portrayal of the "still youngish" prince is now balanced structurally in the story by the portrayal of this twenty-five-year-old woman. The narrator has previously seen her only from a distance, and has imagined her as "something special" with her wealth. In his conversation with the princess, the narrator learns that although she is actually not physically attractive—she is "ugly, short, scraggy and round-shouldered"—she is intelligent, with magnificent hair, and a "look of culture" in her pure face. When the narrator makes his request to be able to shoot, the princess refuses him until the name of the prince is mentioned. Then she looks out in the yard and sees him. Chekhov's description of the delight and the suffering that make her "ugly face" radiant is masterful. The story closes with the narrator's receiving permission from the princess to shoot. The overall structure of the story is finely balanced: all the elements of the narrative are essential, so that the plot has remarkable clearness of line.[29]

After 1887, Chekhov placed more emphasis on character development and less on complexity of plot, prompting the term "formless" to be applied to his stories. Although the term is not accurate—the form is simply altered, not nonexistent—it does indicate Chekhov's gradual shift from an insistence on objective narration to an interest in a closer, more subtle narration. One story from this period that points in this direction is "Ivan Matveyitch" (Garnett), in which a man of learning dictates an article to the young man of the title. Since Ivan is late in arriving for the dictation, the learned man is irritable and threatens to fire him. But at the close of the story, after Ivan talks of how birds and spiders are caught in his homeland, he asks Ivan to remain to visit after the dictation. The need for mutual companionship between these two characters, so unlike each other, brings them together. This simple action is apparently so uneventful that the shape of the story seems "formless," but in his subtle way, Chekhov is capturing the essence of these two individuals in a manner new to short fiction.

The Protagonist's Voice, 1888–1894

From 1888 on, Chekhov usually focuses on the protagonist's consciousness, so a typical story is structurally centered in what the protagonist
feels and thinks. A. P. Chudakov notes that the same approach had been
employed by Russian writers from Pushkin to Tolstoy, but Chekhov
used this method as the major structural device in so many of his
narratives that it is most closely associated with him (62). This approach,
in which the story is told almost exclusively through the perception of
the protagonist, is a radical shift from his earlier technique of avoiding
depicting the protagonist's state of mind and of suggesting his thoughts
and feelings only through his actions (Yarmolinsky, 37). The portrayal of
the protagonist's thoughts ultimately resulted in a study of the state of
man's consciousness in the modern world, an achievement M. H. Shot-
ton views as the central aspect of Chekhov's mature work.[30]

The Steppe

Chekhov's first significant fiction from this period is "The Steppe: The
Story of a Journey" (Hingley), a professionally and artistically transitional work. With "The Steppe," Chekhov received his first national
recognition as a serious writer, for it was published by *The Northern Herald*
(Severny vestnik), his first appearance in a high-brow literary journal.
This novella, an account of the journey of a nine-year-old boy through
southern Russia, represents a culmination of Chekhov's series of stories
with child protagonists. The thoughts and feelings of Yegorushka are
presented with Chekhov's special insight into the child's mind. The boy
is traveling by wagon across the steppe to attend school in a city. On the
journey, Yegorushka encounters the people who inhabit this vast open
country: the wagoners, or "carters," of the wagon trains, the landowners
with large estates, the innkeepers, and the isolated farmers.

The description of the countryside and of the people is Chekhov's
major accomplishment. Passages with particular force portray the child's
terror in a violent thunderstorm and the campfire-side story-telling
scenes. The visual imagery of the prose suggests a series of rich, realistic

paintings, but this long story is formally flawed. The various characters and incidents do not build on one another into a focused, overall design. Although individual scenes have a vivid, lyric intensity, they do not coalesce into an organic whole. Although flawed, "The Steppe" is Chekhov's first mature attempt at the novella, which he went on to do with considerable success in this period with "The Duel" and "Ward Number Six."

Stories of the Authentic Life and Moral Ambiguity in Domestic Settings

Chekhov's next story to appear in the prestigious *The Northern Herald*, "Lights" (Hingley), is a transitional work in terms of subject. Between 1888 and 1894, most of Chekhov's stories explore philosophical issues. In exploring these problems, he actually was ascribing to the nineteenth-century Russian utilitarian view of fiction. Often his protagonists are living lives based on falsehood—empty, unacceptable lives. In existential terms, they live inauthentic lives, contrary to their basic beliefs. "Lights" develops that subject of the authentic life, one of Chekhov's major concerns during the remainder of his writing life.

In form, "Lights" marks a return to the more highly focused short story. Only one third as long as "The Steppe," it contains a story within a story. The frame story is established when a doctor on his rounds in the steppe country encounters a railway engineer and his assistant. The doctor spends an evening with them during which the engineer, Ananyev, relates a story from his young manhood, the inner story. The engineer tells this story for the benefit of his assistant, a pessimistic student who does not believe in the value of their work. The story concerns Ananyev's conversion from being a man who had neither convictions nor a definite moral code, "neither heart nor reason" (IV, 227), to a man who recognizes the inauthenticity of his life and then embraces a life of productivity as a functioning member of society. Ananyev now believes in his fellow man, in the value of work, and in family.

The incident that leads to his conversion occurs when Ananyev is a young man of twenty-six, when he meets a former high school sweetheart named Kitty, now married to a man she does not love. Ananyev recognizes that Kitty is a well-meaning and loving young woman, but that she is emotionally "tortured" by the circumstances of her provincial life—a theme Chekhov has developed in previous stories—so she feels she has nothing to live for. Kitty is experiencing the same dispiriting boredom and dissatisfaction with her life that appeared earlier in "The Chemist's Wife," a boredom that eventually leads to despair. Ananyev takes sexual advantage of her situation, and although Kitty thereby feels a happiness she has never known before, the experience has little meaning for him. Promising to meet her again, Ananyev instead leaves town. A few days later, however, he comes to sense a deeper significance in his experience with Kitty, and returns to beg her forgiveness. This pattern of a man noncommittedly seducing a woman and then realizing later the deeper significance of the union was to reappear a dozen years later in the masterpiece, "A Lady with a Dog."

Returning to the frame—the outer story of the doctor's visit—Chekhov places Ananyev's conversion in perspective. The student is unmoved by the story, and responds that a person must be "very naïve if one believes in human thought and logic, and attaches overriding significance to humanity" (IV, 230). When the doctor leaves the next morning, his final thought and the closing of the story is that "nothing in this world makes sense" (IV, 233). But Ananyev's compelling story overshadows these responses, and develops those Tolstoian ideals Chekhov previously explored in "An Encounter" and "The Beggar." In "Lights," however, the scope is widened so the theme of the meaningless and inauthentic life is integrated with the theme of modern boredom and despair, a direction Chekhov was to follow in a number of his remaining stories. "Lights" is a watershed work; succeeding stories deal with the subject of the inauthentic life either in domestic settings or in the world at large, outside conjugal or family relationships.

Among the most accomplished of Chekhov's domestic stories on the subject of the inauthentic life is "The Party" (Hingley).[31] In contrast to "The Steppe," the story is a model in form, a fully developed, densely symbolic, and highly focused narrative. For sharpness of narrative focus, "The Party" can be compared to "Easter Eve" and "A Trivial Incident." The rhythms and language of the narrative are exactly suited to the thought processes of the protagonist, Olga.

The events are experienced entirely through Olga's consciousness so her thoughts and feelings become the structural center of the action. The events revolve around the name-day party of Olga's husband, a young judge. Seven months pregnant as the story opens, Olga is emotionally and physically weary from entertaining. Although the couple are financially well established, her husband's reactionary political views have created tension with some members of the community. He is against trial by jury and university education for women, although Olga herself is university educated. As the day drags out, she forces herself to act the part of the charming hostess, although she is increasingly aware of the hypocrisy of her situation.

The crisis occurs after the guests leave. Olga is consumed by the desperate boredom and triviality of her life and argues with her husband. She declares that they both have been leading "dishonest lives," lives she can no longer tolerate. The dynamics and complexity of the marital relationship are superbly portrayed. Olga is both irrationally repelled by the good looks of her husband, and drawn to him through the power of their love. At the height of the argument, Olga begins to miscarry. Chekhov uses his experience as a physician in describing Olga's pain and confusion as she is given chloroform for an operation. The story closes with Olga waking to find her husband in despair over the loss of the baby, while she herself feels spiritually drained and numb with apathy. Another example of Chekhov's foresight is the portrayal of one problem Olga faces: she is an educated woman without an opportunity to employ or enjoy her education, living with a man who believes in a male-dominated world.

Chekhov's next attempt at exploring the authentic life in a domestic setting is "A Dreary Story—From An Old Man's Memoirs" (Hingley). D. S. Mirsky believes this story marks the beginning of Chekhov's mature period; the characters' mutual isolation and growing disillusionment characterize what came to be known as the "Chekhovian state of mind" (59–60). In contrast to "The Party," the protagonist of "A Dreary Story" is a man, a sixty-two-year old professor of medical science who, in his own opinion, leads a bleak life. His cranky but intelligent, complex and self-centered first-person narration marks a new dimension for Chekhov. The professor believes he has only a few months to live, and this situation has forced him to question his entire outlook on life. The news has taken the joy and significance out of his life's work. At one time he was a happy man who loved his research and colleagues, but he no longer possesses the concentration required to lecture. In the middle of class, tears often choke him as he experiences a "furious, hysterical urge" to communicate his despair to his students. In these feelings of distraction, desperation, fear, and pain, the professor's situation resembles that of Ivan Ilych in Tolstoy's "The Death of Ivan Ilych" (1886).

The professor believes a person is defined by his desires. He realizes in his desires—for "wives, children, friends and pupils" to love one other as ordinary people—there is some missing element. This element, which is "something vital, something really basic" (V, 80), would bind his separate thoughts into one organic whole, and would enable him to live an authentic life. The professor's desire for people to simply love one other is admirable, but this ideal is a world away from his daily life, filled with dissatisfaction and despair, feelings which are manifested most strongly in his domestic life. He is regularly insomniac, and once, when his wife attempts to comfort him, wonders in amazement that the slim woman whom he once loved so deeply because of her "good, clear brain, her pure heart, her beauty" has become "this fat, clumsy" old woman who is a painful sight to him. Life at home is unbearably boring, particularly since his daughter became engaged to a young man he finds distasteful. Although he once lived at home with a "real family," the professor now feels the "lunch guest of a spurious wife" and daughter; a great change has occurred, but he missed its process, and has no clue as to its cause. The professor, confronted with his own dissatisfaction, transfers the blame to the members of his family.

He spends his most agreeable hours outside his home in the company of a young woman, Katya, for whom he has served as guardian since the death of her father. Katya suffers from a boredom and malaise that matches the professor's. A failed actress, she feels she is a "negative phenomenon," someone whose life does not add up to anything. The climax occurs when Katya goes to the professor in despair and begs for his help. The professor can no more help her than he can help himself, so she leaves for good. For all his success in the world at large, he is a failure in his domestic and human relationships. He is a man isolated by his inability to maintain meaningful ties with others, a condition generated by his self-centered view of life.

D. S. Mirsky views "A Dreary Story" as beginning a succession of masterpieces of the 1890s, with "The Duel" (Hingley), the longest story of Chekhov's mature period, next in line (360–361).[32] Like "A Dreary Story," "The Duel" focuses on the effort to live an authentic life within the domestic setting, but here the point of view does not remain confined to the consciousness of the protagonist, Ivan Layevsky, but rather rotates among characters. Those chapters portraying the consciousness of Nadezhda, Layevsky's lover, are of particular importance.

Inspired by Tolstoy's ideal of the return to nature, Layevsky has fled St. Petersburg with Nadezhda, another man's wife, planning to become a farmer in the Caucasus. But instead Layevsky has worked as a government clerk, abandoning Tolstoy's ideal, and has grown weary of

Nadezhda. He has come to realize that, instead of running away from the emptiness of their lives among the intelligentsia in St. Petersburg, Nadezhda and he were simply running away from her husband. He views himself as a "superfluous man" (*lishniy chelovek*)—a man for whom society has no place. The concept of the superfluous man has a tradition in Russian literature, and Layevsky uses this label to avoid coming to terms with his life.

Nadezhda is living a life as inauthentic as Layevsky's. She sees herself as the only beautiful, intellectual woman in the town, but also senses that, in the depth of her being, she is a "petty, vulgar, worthless, insignificant woman." Although she loves Layevsky, she entertains the local police inspector when Layevsky is at work to relieve the boredom of her life. Nadezhda's lack of self-direction, self-determination, and will power places her in a false position so that she grows to despise herself.

The third significant character in the novella is Von Koren, a zoologist. One of the primary conflicts in the novella revolves around Von Koren's disapproval of Layevsky. Von Koren, as a scientist, represents the new progressive way of thinking about society, but he pushes his views to the extreme, declaring that people like Layevsky are parasites on society and either should be forced to do hard labor or should be exterminated. In his extremist application of the laws of natural selection to human beings, Von Koren is a precursor of the German Nazism of the 1930s.

Layevsky, aware of Von Koren's attitude toward him, believes that men like Von Koren are tyrants who act in the name of improving the human race. They are the kind of men who would "post eunuchs to guard over chastity and morality" and would "give orders to fire at anyone who stepped outside the circle of our narrow, conservative morality" (V, 173). Borrowing the terms of Alberto Moravia, one can argue that these characters, like all characters in longer stories, come to represent ideologies, become symbols of ideas beyond themselves.[33] Von Koren and Layevsky play out the struggle between the superfluous man and the man of science.

Layevsky senses some truth in Von Koren's criticism, for he is aware of the inauthentic nature of his life. He admits his life is based on "lies, laziness and cowardice," and declares that he at times hates and despises himself. He longs for a transformation, for the new life so many Chekhov characters come to desire, and this transformation occurs when Von Koren forces Layevsky to a duel. The duel forces Layevsky to a kind of conversion, a realignment of his inner moral nature. This conversion resembles the experience of the engineer in "Lights," although here it is worked through in more specific detail. The realignment of a character's moral nature is a key element in many of Chekhov's stories of the inauthentic life during this period. Because short fiction usually patterns itself around some change in the protagonist, conversion is a natural focus for the form.

In the story published immediately following "The Duel," the subject of living an authentic life within a domestic setting is once again a central concern. In "My Wife" (Hingley) Chekhov returns to the first-person narrator, once again an unsympathetic figure. A retired engineer, Paul Asorin now spends his time writing a history of railroads in Russia. The central conflict of the story involves his relationship with his estranged wife Natalie, who continues to live in the same house with him. Although Asorin adores her, he cannot control his urges to belittle and control her. In past years, their arguments have left them irresistibly attracted to each other, but now Natalie wants to break completely with him. The portrayal of their relationship is Chekhov's most impressive accomplishment in this story.

After Asorin agrees to leave Natalie for good, he drives to a neighbor's estate where he undergoes a sort of conversion, like the engineer in "Lights" and Layevsky in "The Duel." Asorin's experience, however, is more limited. When he asks his neighbor for an honest opinion of him, the neighbor replies Asorin is an impressive man in appearance and bearing, that he is clever, and that he is a hard worker, but that he hasn't "really got a soul." The word "soul" is not used in its traditional religious definition: the neighbor refers to the ability of a man to respond sensitively to life's experiences, the beautiful and the tragic, the wonderful and the sublime. Asorin's inauthentic life has made him an emotionally impoverished man, like the professor in "A Dreary Story." Asorin returns home to Natalie, but unlike the engineer in "Lights" and Layevsky in "The Duel," whose good works are apparent in their lives after their conversions, Asorin does not become a productive member of society. His conversion is a less radical realignment of his inner moral nature.

"The Butterfly" (Hingley), one of Chekhov's most widely translated stories, once again focuses on a married couple: a newly wed junior doctor, Dymov, and his attractive twenty-two-year-old bride, Olga. Chekhov often subjects those characters of whom he does not approve to critical irony, and none comes under sharper criticism than Olga, who spends her days attempting to befriend celebrities. She also surrounds herself with artists—writers, painters, musicians—who have nothing in common with her husband. Her polar opposite, Dymov, one of Chekhov's virtuous doctor figures, works tirelessly at two hospitals while writing his master's thesis. The strength of the story is its clarity of line; the events and characters are balanced perfectly against one another. Chekhov eschews his usual ambiguity when the superficial Olga drifts into an affair with a painter and Dymov suffers the situation in silence. In contrast to most of Chekhov's stories from this period, the narration is omniscient, usually remaining at that objective distance which allows for irony and moving into Olga's thoughts only when it becomes necessary to portray her feelings.

In the last section of the story, the narration is centered in Olga's experience as she undergoes a variation of the conversion common to many of Chekhov's characters. Dymov catches diphtheria from his patients, and during his suffering, Olga realizes the nature of the inauthentic life she has been living. As Dymov lies dying, the attending physicians comment on what a remarkable man he is; Olga suddenly realizes that Dymov is a great man compared with everyone else she has known, and adores him now in a manner she never had before. His death underscores the irony of her situation.

In contrast to the clarity of plot line in "The Butterfly," Chekhov's next major story to explore domestic life is without a clear-cut hero or villain. More complex in its treatment of character, "Neighbors" (Hingley) looks forward to the works of Chekhov's last period, in which his protagonists are more true to life, neither wholly good nor wholly bad, their lives morally ambiguous, their moral choices complex.

The story depicts a bachelor whose familial relationships are the center of his life. Ivashin lives with his mother, his aunt, and his younger sister. His tranquil life is disturbed when his sister moves in with a neighboring landowner who is married already, although his estranged wife no longer lives at the estate. Morally outraged at his sister's behavior, Ivashin decides to confront her and the landowner about their cohabitation. In the process of his visit, however, Ivashin is confronted with the complexities of his moral judgment: although he disapproves of his sister's living with a married man, he realizes she is happy, and instead of condemning the couple as he'd planned, Ivashin tells them he will visit occasionally, suggesting that he sympathizes with the cohabitation.

As Ivashin returns home, he stops to gaze into a pond and he experiences an epiphany in which he realizes that he has not done nor said what he really intended, and that others have "repaid him in like coin, which was why all life now seemed as dark as this pond with its reflection of the night sky and its tangled water-weed" (VI, 117). Ivashin believes the previous occupants of the landowner's estate had solved their problems with direct action—in one instance, a man was flogged to death in the dining room. But such direct action is not possible in Ivashin's "tangled" moral world, a world as twisted and unclear as the dark, weed-choked pond before him. Ivashin, a modern hero, will now live forever in moral ambiguity.

After "Neighbors," Chekhov's next major work is a full-length novella that again explores similar themes. Ronald Hingley calls "An Anonymous Story" (Hingley) "magnificent" and believes it is possibly Chekhov's finest work of fiction (VI, 11). Like "A Dreary Story" and "My Wife," the point of view in "An Anonymous Story" is first person. But unlike the narrators in those previous stories, this protagonist is a sympathetic character; in fact, his compassionate nature becomes a key factor in the story's development. The narrator, an unlikely hero for Chekhov, is a radical revolutionary activist who has gone underground to stalk a prominent politician, a serious enemy of his revolutionary cause, in order to assassinate him. To accomplish his mission, the narrator has secured a position as the footman to the politician's son, Orlov, a civil servant in St. Petersburg. Although the narrator learns nothing from Orlov, he does become deeply involved in Orlov's life, which significantly changes his own revolutionary aims.

Orlov, who leads an inauthentic life, as self-centered as the protagonists in "A Dreary Story" and "My Wife," is a cynic, a very intelligent and world-wise man, but one who has no ideals, no strong moral base. The narrator believes the reason Orlov plays cards so frequently is to hide the "shattering, abysmal boredom" of his life from himself and others. Zinaida, an attractive young woman, leaves her husband to live with Orlov. She believes she is beginning a new life and permanent relationship with Orlov, but he secretly views the relationship quite differently. Having no desire for a traditional domestic establishment, Orlov prefers to retain his old habits and freedom, his peace of mind and his privacy secure. Although Zinaida has made a permanent commitment to Orlov, he believes such cohabitation can last no more than a few years, regardless of how intensely they love each other. Some of the best writing in the novella is in the portrayal of the tension between Orlov and Zinaida as their relationship begins to deteriorate and Zinaida slowly discovers Orlov's real position. During these scenes, the narrator begins to fall in love with Zinaida, and, in a typically Chekhovian irony, the narrator desires just the situation Orlov detests: "a wife, a nursery, garden paths, and a little cottage" (VI, 211). The narrator's feelings for Zinaida foreshadow a transformation in his life that occurs during an unexpected visit by Orlov's father, the politician.

During this visit, the narrator has an excellent opportunity to assassinate the father. But unexpectedly, he finds himself responding to the father without his former hatred, viewing him instead as simply another old man nearing a natural death. This experience works a conversion in the narrator, much like the conversions of the engineer in "Lights," Layevsky in "The Duel," and Asorin in "My Wife." Like the engineer in "Lights," the narrator suddenly feels filled with potential and a desire to work for the betterment of mankind. Although the protagonist never achieves much scope as a functioning member of society, he eventually does lead a meaningful life in his own terms, loving and caring for Zinaida's infant daughter by Orlov after her suicide.

After two years, however, the narrator becomes terminally ill and must go to Orlov to request that he serve as the little girl's guardian. The final action in the novella provides a closing comment on the difference between the narrator and Orlov: although Orlov is the biological father of the little girl, he does not have the narrator's capacity to love the child. He will accept financial responsibility, but will not keep her in his own living quarters where her presence would interfere with his life-style. Thus, Orlov is incapable of living an authentic life.

Robert Louis Jackson terms "A Woman's Kingdom" (Hingley) an "artistic masterpiece in every respect."[34] Certainly it is one of Chekhov's two or three most successful novellas in terms of artistic unity, and the character of Anne Glagolev, a twenty-five-year old woman who owns a large factory, is one of Chekhov's most sympathetic heroines. She not only embodies Chekhov's moral concerns, but her good humor and sharp intelligence complement her integrity. Like a number of protagonists from this period, Anne senses she is living a false life and desires to transform it, to change her present existence for one of freedom and happiness. The significant action of the novella is psychological, centered in Anne's mind and involving her thoughts and emotions.

The time frame of the story is highly focused, occurring over the course of a roughly twenty-four-hour period, during Christmas Eve and Christmas Day. In fact, "A Woman's Kingdom" is a crowning achievement in Chekhov's series of Christmas stories. As the action opens, Anne has received an unexpectedly large settlement from a lawsuit, and is deciding how to help the poor of the community with some of the money. On an impulse, she resolves to deliver personally a portion of the sum to an unemployed clerk with a sick wife and five small daughters. But her attempt at Christian charity ends in frustration when Anne discovers the clerk is an alcoholic who will buy drink instead of helping his family. The scene in which Anne gives the clerk the money resembles the compelling depictions of the suffering of destitute families in Dostoevsky's novels. Anne, whose father was a factory worker, lived in housing similar to that of the alcoholic clerk, so she feels she must attempt to help, despite her belief that her efforts will count for nothing. The moral ambiguity of her situation is defined by this paradoxical response. Although Anne feels a deep responsibility toward the members of her community, especially her employees, her unease over that feeling is one of the factors that contribute to her sense of living a false existence.

During the visit to the clerk's lodging Anne meets Pimenov, one of the workers at her factory. She is strongly attracted to this man with his self-confident physical bearing, and he represents a possible marriage choice for her. He would provide the conventional domestic life for which she yearns. Much of the psychological action of the novella revolves around Anne's thoughts about the possibility of this marriage. In Anne's luxurious house, during a Christmas reception for various workers at her factory and members of the community, Anne has the opportunity to observe Pimenov further, now within a social setting. After his departure, Anne has a lengthy conversation with her lawyer, Victor Lysevich. Although he is a wealthy and "remarkably healthy" bachelor of forty-two to whom she feels quite close, the lawyer does not wish to marry. As a sophisticated man of society, however, he represents the polar opposite of Pimenov. Lysevich encourages Anne to live a freer life, to indulge herself, even to take lovers if she wishes. But Anne, with her conventional morals, recoils from his suggestions.

However, during their conversation, Lysevich discusses modern literature, a subject that interests Anne. Afterwards, she impulsively gives him the money she received in the lawsuit as a Christmas bonus. The action is one indication of Anne's underlying false position: Lysevich does not deserve the money—in fact, she knows he has cheated her in the past—but giving him the money seems to solve her problem of just what to do with it. Later that night, alone in her room, she finally decides Pimenov would never fit into her life, for he would seem "pathetic and helpless" in the required social situations. She weeps from shame and boredom, deciding it is really too late for her to "devise some new, special mode of existence" (VII, 90). Unlike the engineer in "Lights" or Layevsky in "The Duel," Anne does not undergo a conversion, but will live on in her present situation. This pattern of the character fervently desiring to change his or her life, and then realizing that such change will not occur, looks forward to Chekhov's later stories and the major plays.

If "A Woman's Kingdom" illustrates the difficulties of a woman's achieving an authentic life within the confines of her professional and domestic life, then "The Russian Master" (Hingley) explores this same basic situation for a man. One of the more accomplished short stories from this period, it illustrates Chekhov's ability to create complexity and depth of character through a few highly selected incidents. Through these incidents, Chekhov portrays first a man's life as he courts, marries, then recognizes that his life has become inauthentic. In the first section of the story, Sergy Nikitin, a teacher, pursues one of the most desirable young women of the community; the section closes as Nikitin falls asleep, "exhausted by bliss," and looks forward to his marriage. This section was published in 1889 as a separate story, "The Mediocrities." As a separate story, however, this first section only suggests that Nikitin's domestic situation will evolve into a quagmire of dissatisfaction and unhappiness.

Chekhov wrote the second section five years later, after he had worked through several other stories with similar themes. The concluding section has a clarity of direction that places the first section in a wider context and provides balance and resonance to the events in both. Through apparently minor incidents of an apparently normal life, Nikitin becomes increasingly dissatisfied with his domestic situation and his professional life. A feeling develops within him that he is deceiving people and is living a life based on falsehood. He begins to long for a very different world, for some obsession to make him oblivious to self, because now his life is "incompatible with peace of mind and personal happiness" (VII, 129). Although Nikitin appears to have every reason to be happy—his marriage brought a large dowry, he is in fine health—he feels "surrounded by smug, complacent mediocrities, dreary nonentities" (VII, 130); he writes in his diary, "I must escape this very day or I shall go out of my mind" (VII, 130). The story closes on that statement; Chekhov once again portrays the problem, but does not offer a solution.

The dramatic inner changes that occur in a person while living an apparently normal life were to become one of Chekhov's major concerns in subsequent fiction. In the novella "Three Years" (Hingley) he goes beyond the recognition dramatized in "The Russian Master." The novella's point of view is not confined to the consciousness of the protagonist Laptev, but revolves among characters, as in "The Duel." Those chapters devoted to Julia, the wife of the protagonist, are of particular importance as she undergoes inner changes that both parallel and work against changes in Laptev. As in so many stories by Chekhov, the relationship between a man and a woman occupies the center stage of the conflict, but, thanks to the larger scope of the novella, that relationship is treated with greater complexity, and over a longer time frame, than is usual in Chekhov.

Laptev perfectly illustrates one kind of Chekhovian hero: the sensitive, inefficient man who cannot overcome his own inertia, a hero developed earlier in the character of Layevsky in "The Duel." Laptev declares he "simply can't adapt to life and master it" (VII, 210), recognizing his own inadequacy. In contrast to the couple in "The Duel," however, Laptev and Julia are mature and responsible. After their marriage, Julia is unhappy but undergoes a significant change when she has their child and lives through a happy time of inner peace. But then the child dies of diphtheria. After a period of mourning, Julia not only becomes interested in life once again, but in Laptev as her husband.

Laptev, however, has resigned himself to a life without happiness, another characteristic of this Chekhovian hero. He tells Julia that, for one night during their courtship, he experienced a "state of bliss," an experience similar to Nikitin's feeling before his marriage at the end of section 1 of "The Russian Master"; but like Nikitin, Laptev has become greatly dissatisfied with life after marriage. In response to Julia's renewed interest in him and to his responsibilities with the family business, Laptev declares "I feel as if our life was over" and "It's as if a dim half-life were beginning" (VII, 220). In Chekhov, this dim half-life, this life of grayness, is the condition of modern man.

In the closing chapter, Laptev comes home one day from work and Julia declares she has grown to love him. As Laptev muses on the changes that have occurred during their three years of marriage, and as he speculates on the changes the future might bring, he notices how attractive Julia is. This closing scene suggests the possibility of a more fulfilling life for both of them. Portraying the changes of these characters over the course of their daily activities, as they evolve toward more authentic lives, is another of Chekhov's significant accomplishments in this work.

Stories on the Meaning of Life

After "Lights," most stories Chekhov wrote can be divided into two groups: first, stories with characters who question the authenticity of their lives as they interact with spouses or other significant figures in domestic settings, as discussed; and second, stories with characters who urgently question the meaning of life—and also often the authenticity of their own lives—in other settings. In this second group of stories, since no spouse exists, another character with whom the protagonist interacts often serves to dramatize the concept of the authentic life.

"In Exile" (Hingley), one of the few stories with a setting inspired by the 1890 journey Chekhov made through Siberia to Sakhalin Island, centers on a dialogue between two convicts. These characters are brought to the same self-questioning as Chekhov's middle-class characters but through very different circumstances. Old Simon is a ferryman who is proud he has survived in exile, an accomplishment achieved through not allowing himself to care about having a wife or a family or freedom. Opposed to him is a young Tartar, a Turkish-speaking Russian recently exiled for horse stealing, who desperately yearns for his wife and home back in his province.

As the two men huddle one cold night at a small fire beside a riverbank, Old Simon tells a story to illustrate how a person must survive in this rugged, desolate land, where ice still flows after Easter in the river beside them. The story concerns an ongoing argument Simon has with a gentleman exiled fifteen years ago for forging a will. Because the gentleman desires a life like he had before, he suffers. Simon has warned the man he must give up his old life, but the man insists he can be happy in Siberia. The man had sent for his wife and daughter, but because of the difficulty of life in the country, his wife soon ran off with another man. For eight years, the man doggedly sought his freedom so he could pursue her, suffering all the time. Now the man's daughter, the "apple of his eye," has developed consumption, and he spends his time chasing doctors. Simon believes the daughter will surely die, in which case the man either will hang himself or will attempt to escape Siberia. If the man attempts to escape, Simon knows he will be caught, flogged, and sent to a hard labor camp. But the Tartar believes the gentleman is right in wanting the life he does, and that Simon is wrong for not desiring such a life. In his halting Russian, the Tartar declares, "You say you don't need nothing. But not need nothing is bad" (VI, 95). To desire might mean suffering, the Tartar concedes, but for the chance of such happiness, the

Tartar would accept "any tortures whatever and would thank God for them" (VI, 95).

The two men sleep on the ground until awakened by the gentleman whom they have been discussing, seeking a doctor for his daughter. After delivering the man to the far bank, the Tartar and Simon argue once again about how to live in the world. The Tartar believes "God made man to be alive, to have joy and grief and sorrow," and since Simon does not want such emotions, he believes Simon is "dead"—"You stone, you clay. Stone need nothing, you need nothing" (VI, 98). The Tartar in broken language expresses a moral position with which Chekhov sympathizes. But Simon, unconvinced by the Tartar's argument, simply goes into a nearby hut to sleep, while the Tartar remains out beside the riverbank, sobbing, making "noises like a hound baying" in his mental suffering. In portraying the sensitivity and the suffering of this ordinary convict, Chekhov creates a masterpiece that Katherine Mansfield termed "incomparable."[35]

The argument over the meaning of life is resumed in a novella Chekhov began writing a few weeks after "In Exile" was completed. "Ward Number Six" (Hingley) is one of his most widely translated works. Ronald Hingley groups the novella with "A Dreary Story," "Peasants," and "A Lady with a Dog" as the select group of Chekhov stories that have made the greatest impact on Russia and the world at large (VI, 15). The two characters who engage in the argument over the nature of the authentic life are Dr. Andrew Ragin, the head physician of a provincial hospital, and Ivan Gromov, a former government official who is now a patient in the hospital's ward for the insane.

Ragin is one of those many Chekhovian characters who began his career with hard work, a sense of self-worth and optimism, but was eventually overcome by the circumstances of his isolated, provincial surroundings. Twenty years before, Ragin saw patients daily and performed operations, but now, overcome by the boring monotony and "palpable futility" of his job, he spends his time reading while the hospital conditions deteriorate. Ragin believes "everything in the world is trivial and boring" except the "higher spiritual manifestations of the human intellect" (VI, 135). Living in his provincial town, lacking intellectual concerns and conversation, has made Ragin's life a "deplorable trap." Although Ragin feels dishonest, knowing people are suffering from the unhygienic conditions in the hospital, he concludes that this feeling does not matter, for he is only part of an "inevitable social evil." Consequently, he believes it is not his fault he is dishonest. Ragin's concept of the meaning of life is essentially a more sophisticated articulation of the view of life espoused by Simon in "In Exile."

Chekhov's accomplishment in the novella is creating complex characters vitally concerned with philosophical ideas. Ragin's thoughts are dramatized one day on his hospital rounds. He engages in conversation with Ivan, who accuses him of being a thief and a charlatan. In response, Ragin attempts to convince Ivan that it really does not matter who is the doctor or the patient, whether Ivan or Ragin: since the laws of nature will remain as they are, Ragin believes, the "real essence of things won't change" (VI, 142). Consistent with his classic stoic philosophy, Ragin maintains Ivan has the two blessings higher than any known to man: "profound speculation on the meaning of life," and "utter contempt for the world's foolish vanities" (VI, 142). Thus he believes Ivan should be happy to live "inside" himself at the ward.

Ivan counters Ragin's argument by declaring he loves life passionately and rejects the stoic philosophy, for a "new day *will* dawn" and justice shall "triumph" (VI, 141). The intellectual exchange stimulates Ragin to seek Ivan out for further conversation, and over the course of several days, the two men have an ongoing dialogue that, as in "In Exile," is the structural center of the story. Ivan cries, "To pain I respond with shouts and tears, meanness makes me indignant, revolting behavior sickens me" (VI, 146); he is a compassionate man "surprised at human depravity." Ivan resembles the Tartar from "In Exile": both men advocate living in the world, experiencing life's emotions. The fact that Ivan is a mental patient and the Tartar a convict adds an additional ironic dimension.

Dr. Ragin, for all his learning, holds essentially the same perspective on life as Old Simon: one should be disengaged. That Chekhov should choose the doctor figure to illustrate how a man who believes in such a philosophy can degenerate into incompetency is a comment on his integrity as an artist: although Chekhov often holds up the doctor figure as a heroic model, he also criticizes the failings of individual medical practitioners. Because of the clearly stated positions of Ragin and Ivan, the novella possesses that same clarity of line found in "The Butterfly" and "In Exile," but with added depth of character.

Like "The Butterfly," the story closes with an ironic twist: because of Ragin's noninvolvement with his provincial world, he is supplanted by another doctor, an ambitious man who confines Ragin in Ward Number Six against his will. In confinement, Ragin, terrified and experiencing pain he cannot philosophize away, undergoes a moral conversion. In an epiphany, he realizes "just such a pain must be the daily lot, year in and year out" of many men (VI, 166), and wonders how it was that for twenty years he ignored this reality. Ragin does not live long with his newfound knowledge, however; he dies of a stroke the following day, the result of a beating administered by the ward guard. With this action, the story doubles back upon itself in an ironic closure.

The subject of the authentic life is also the theme of "Rothschild's Fiddle" (Hingley). This highly focused short story is narrated by a voice separate from the consciousness of the protagonist, a mode that became pronounced in the stories during Chekhov's last period, from 1895 to 1904. This masterpiece illustrates Chekhov's compassionate attitude toward his characters as well as any story he wrote. In contrast to "In Exile" and "Ward Number Six," the protagonist in this story does not argue directly with an antagonist but he does come to recognize the inauthentic nature of his life and undergo a moral conversion, triggered by the death of his wife.

Jacob, a coffin maker, loses his wife of fifty years to typhoid fever. After her funeral, he realizes how inhumanely he treated her during their marriage, for it now seems he no more noticed her than he did a "cat or dog." Through this portrayal of Jacob's awareness of his indifference toward his wife, Chekhov generates sympathy for the character. In his grief, Jacob wanders down to a river where he used to spend time with his wife and daughter. This daughter had died in a past so far removed from the present that he had forgotten her. On the riverbank, Jacob has an epiphany in which he realizes his life had "flowed past without profit, without enjoyment—gone aimlessly, leaving nothing to show for it" (VI, 99). Because of the inauthentic nature of his past life, Jacob realizes that his "future was empty." He develops an awareness of the humanness of people in which he not only questions his ill treatment of his wife, but his mistreatment of a Jew named Rothschild. Jacob, who occasionally plays the fiddle in a Jewish band, is anti-Semitic, "obsessed with hatred and contempt for Jews," and in particular, he despises Rothschild, whom he had insulted before his walk down to the riverbank. But after this epiphany, when Rothschild approaches him again, Jacob treats him with compassion.

Shortly afterward, when Jacob himself is dying from typhoid fever, he plays his fiddle with a great poignancy, a poignancy which Rothschild is able to recapture afterwards in his own playing. At Jacob's death, his moral conversion complete, he leaves Rothschild his fiddle in a gesture that symbolizes the compassion that has developed out of his suffering.

Charles May observes that Chekhov's pathos in this story is set in an objective, ironically comic mode closely resembling the tales of Bernard Malamud (1914–86).[36]

In "Gusev" (Hingley), another masterpiece written four years previously in 1890, the spiritual dimension takes a more mystical, enigmatic turn than in "Rothschild's Fiddle." Again, the characters are working-class people, and again, illness and suffering are the central events. Gusev is a discharged soldier, a peasant dying from consumption in a ship's sick bay. Gusev's peasant mythology represents one view of the nature of life. As in "Ward Number Six" and "In Exile," a second character, in this case Paul Ivanovich, a fellow patient in the sick bay, voices a different view. When Gusev explains rough seas as "the wind breaking loose from its chain" and expresses fear that a huge fish will sink the ship, Paul Ivanovich reprimands him for not using his "reason." These characters are ideologically opposed: Paul Ivanovich represents a critical, rational view of life and Gusev an irrational acceptance of life as it is. Paul Ivanovich has moved from place to place protesting against social hypocrisy, living a "conscious life." Chekhov himself practiced this rational approach to living. Outside the context of the story, Chekhov clearly was sympathetic to Paul Ivanovich's position, but, as an artist with an eye for verisimilitude and integrity of character, he does not make Paul Ivanovich a particularly attractive person. Even Paul Ivanovich himself admits his uncompromising personality tries his friends. Nor is Gusev in the tradition of the noble savage. He has a brutal aspect to his character, which surfaces in his desire to give a "good clout on the neck" to people when he is bored (V, 106). Paul Ivanovich is in much greater mental and physical pain than Gusev; however, he can "endure hell" and has a "critical attitude" toward his illness that enables him to face it better. He believes Gusev remains in "darkness," experiencing the terribleness of his illness to a much greater degree than he does. But, ironically, Paul Ivanovich dies first. After his death, another man in the sick bay comments that Paul Ivanovich was a "restless man," for he could not make peace with his world.

In contrast, Gusev's thoughts are relatively serene. Recurring, pleasant images of his peasant farm flow in and out of his mind in Chekhov's lyric passages. The images are so pleasant that Gusev's happiness "takes his breath away." However, one disturbing image reappears for "no reason whatever": a large bull's head without eyes—Chekhov's startling, enigmatic symbol of death. The depiction of Gusev's mind in this feverish state marks a development from such earlier stories of altered states of consciousness as "Typhus" and "Sleepy." Chekhov's medical experience once again helps him to create the altered mind with verisimilitude with his compelling impressionistic sense of character.

Chekhov's handling of point of view is brilliant; he shifts in the last section of the story to an omniscient persona, allowing him to relate the events after Gusev's death and burial at sea. Chekhov continues to refer to the body by name, following Gusev underwater where he is swayed by currents and tossed about by fish. The story closes with a final passage on the sunset's painting the clouds brilliant colors. The ocean is personified, scowling at the clouds at first, then taking on itself "tender, joyous, ardent hues for which human speech hardly has a name" (V, 114). The mystical nature of this passage is rather atypical of Chekhov. Although Gusev as a character is in line with Chekhov's peasants, the lyric intensity of this final passage sets the story apart as a masterpiece of powerful simplicity. V. S. Pritchett calls the story an "extraordinary leap" of Chekhov's imagination.[37]

Another story which explores the spiritual dimension of life is "The Student" (Hingley), which Chekhov claimed was one of his favorites (VII, 235). As in "A Nightmare" and "The Letter," the protagonist is a religious man, a seminary student. But instead of emphasizing the protagonist's social position, or his fidelity or weakness, Chekhov directly portrays his spiritual state. Again, the story involves peasant figures, characters of strong emotions capable of responding in an open manner. Appropriately enough, the story, one of Chekhov's Easter stories, takes place on Good Friday. Out hunting, the student reflects on the "ferocious" poverty and hunger, and the "ignorance and misery" of the past thousand years, and decides that situation will continue for another thousand years. While walking home, he comes across two peasant women in the village gardens, seated around their campfire in the middle of the plowed land on a cold evening in which everything seems abandoned and "very gloomy." These two figures, an old widow and her daughter, whose husband beats her, vividly represent the sad situation of humanity on which the student has been reflecting. Chekhov's art in this story is in portraying the landscape and the people with details that mirror the student's mood. The narration is focused in the consciousness of the student, appropriately enough since the change which structures the story and gives form to the events occurs in the student's mind.

After engaging the women in conversation, the student tells the story of Christ's passion and death, relating the events with such directness and open simplicity that the mother weeps. Tears "large and profuse" flow down her cheeks, and the daughter becomes distressed and tense from the story "as if she were holding back a terrible pain" (VII, 107). Later, as the student walks home, he decides it was not his gift for poignant narrative that had moved the women, but the nature of the Easter story itself, and the thought brings him joy. In a brief epiphany, he realizes the past is "linked to the present by an unbroken chain of happenings, each flowing from the other" (VII, 107). In this epiphany, he feels that he has "just seen both ends of that chain": "When he touched one end the other vibrated" (VII, 107). This vision of his place in the world reaffirms his spiritual vocation. He reflects on the role of truth and beauty in a man's life, and decides they are the most important elements. This experience generates the feeling that life is "enchanting, miraculous, imbued with exalted significance" (VII, 108). The gloom of the opening is thus transformed into a transcendent "strange, mysterious happiness," one of the most optimistic endings in Chekhov's work.

Stories of Subjective versus Objective Reality

In "The Student" the protagonist's inner, subjective view of the world manifests itself in the objective, social reality of the two peasant women. More common in Chekhov's stories is the opposite pattern, whereby the subjective views of the protagonists conflict with the social reality. The pattern in these stories is a variation on such stories as "Ward Number Six" and "Rothschild's Fiddle," wherein the characters question the meaning of their lives; the key difference is that these protagonists do not undergo a moral conversion toward self-unity and psychological health, but instead experience a mental breakdown of varying degrees. In the process of this breakdown, the protagonist's state of mind becomes altered, a situation that had interested Chekhov as a student of medicine and as an author in a number of earlier stories, from "Oysters" onward.

Suzanne Ferguson suggests that the protagonist in such impressionistic works as Chekhov's juxtaposes his intuitive, subjective sense of truth with traditional reality.[38] This conflict is formulated differently by Vladimir Kataev in his study of Chekhovian comedy: the conflict manifests itself between the "anguished, weeping, inarticulate and unorderly real life" of the protagonist on the one hand, and the "self-satisfied assurance of established signs and those who use and cherish them" in the objective, social reality on the other.[39] Kataev believes this conflict is the foundation of Chekhov's funniest as well as his most tragic stories and ensures "the profound internal unity of Chekhov's work throughout his career" (67).

One of the stories from this period that emphasizes this conflict is "An Awkward Business" (Hingley), written shortly after the transitional work, "Lights." Yarmolinsky comments that "An Awkward Business" has more substance than many of Chekhov's stories, and that its "psychological acuteness" is typical of Chekhov.[40] Also typical is the point of view, third person centered in the protagonist's consciousness. In many ways, the story is a precursor of "Ward Number Six," written four years later: both stories feature doctor figures forced to examine the nature of their lives. As the physician at a provincial community hospital, Dr. Ovchinnikov struggles to serve the ill. Hospital conditions are poor, and he is haggard and nervous from overwork, regularly treating up to forty-five outpatients a day after his hospital rounds. His efforts resemble those of the young Dr. Ragin, who at first did work hard in similarly difficult conditions; however, before the action in "Ward Number Six" begins, twenty years at the hospital had overcome Dr. Ragin, and he had given up. But Dr. Ovchinnikov, at the hospital eight years, not only treats the ill but also continues his research on medical statistics and maintains a keen interest in social problems.

The dramatic conflict begins when the doctor conducts his hospital rounds and his elderly assistant, not only incompetent but hung over, protests a rebuke from the doctor. Frustrated, the doctor hits the man in the face without realizing what he is doing. Afterwards, the doctor wishes to "put things right" with the assistant, but cannot think of the means to do so. When the assistant, to retain his position, attempts to apologize, the doctor insists that the assistant sue him. In the subsequent hearing, the doctor tells the judge that he has worked until he is ill. The constant irritations of his job, the "trifles and pinpricks," are so numerous his whole life now consists of them, "as a mountain may consist of grains of sand" (IV, 111). The doctor declares he is at the end of his patience. He cannot concentrate properly, for his mind is becoming altered from the stress. This modern theme of the small problems in life mounting up until they are unmanageable is one which Chekhov was among the first to explore.

The chairman of the hospital board resolves the suit out of court, and the doctor despairs at the "attitude to life"—which represents the objective social reality—the chairman and the judge exhibit. The conflict does not end with the doctor's moral conversion; instead he simply reflects on how "everything had fizzled out in a finale so banal." This resolution of the outer, dramatic conflict is typical of the new, "plotless" story that Chekhov was developing. In this new kind of story, although the surface events contain an outer, dramatic conflict, Chekhov's deeper focus is on the inner, psychological action.

When the doctor returns to his hospital, everyone pretends that nothing had happened, including the doctor himself. The doctor's subjective vision of the truth has dissolved in the face of the social reality of this provincial world. However, the idea of "the crass stupidity" of life now becomes a dominant thought for the doctor and serves as a closure to the psychological action of the story. It echoes the final thought of the doctor in "Lights": "No, indeed, nothing in the world makes sense" (IV, 233). Both doctors' comments on the senselessness of life illustrate their inability to reconcile their subjective concept of truth with the objective reality of society.

The effect of stress on the protagonist's mind is developed further in "A Nervous Breakdown" (Hingley), which Chekhov wrote later in 1888. Again, the psychological stress develops from the difference between the character's subjective view of truth and the objective social reality. A more widely known story with its clarity of line and sharp focus, "A Nervous Breakdown" nevertheless lacks the subtle artistic accomplishment of "An Awkward Business." The protagonist, Vasilyev, a sensitive law student, shares the moral vision of the doctor in "An Awkward Business." One night Vasilyev accompanies a medical student and an art student to a Moscow brothel, where his subjective view of the nature of man is tested by a social reality he has not previously experienced. When Vasilyev observes the people there, he feels in "another, utterly peculiar, alien, incomprehensible world" (IV, 166)—a world in which he does not know how to behave. The women and the other brothel employees seem like savages and animals to him; although he struggles to view them as human, he feels only revulsion.

But Vasilyev's loathing gives way to sensations of acute pity for the brothel women and anger at the brothel customers when he overhears a woman crying in the next room with "the heartfelt sobs of the grievously ill-used," and he realizes that these women are "genuine human beings who were ill-treated, who suffered, who wept, and who called for help like people anywhere else" (IV, 169). In his brief epiphany Vasilyev recognizes that certain people believe they represent humanity at its finest—as "great artists and scholars"—and yet exploit "hunger, ignorance and stupidity" by patronizing brothels. This perception brings

Vasilyev's experience into clear conformity with his previous moral view of the world. But the adjustment is short-lived; the overwhelming reality of depravity rises again so that Vasilyev's subjective view of truth is "utterly smashed," and he suddenly feels "childishly scared." Fleeing the establishment, he fancies "the denizens of this weird, mysterious world wanted to chase him, beat him and shower him with obscenities" (IV, 169). The experience alters his mind; out on the street he becomes afraid of the dark, afraid of the snow, and afraid of the lamplight, and "unaccountable, craven fear took possession of him" (IV, 172).

The hysteria Vasilyev feels on fleeing the brothel foreshadows Layevsky's hysteria in "The Duel," written three years later. Both characters come into conflict with larger social realities. The basic difference between the two characters is that Layevsky's inner logic is basically self-serving, whereas Vasilyev's reflects a system of positive moral values.

Vasilyev recognizes he is undergoing a mental breakdown and, as an educated man, attempts to fight his despair with the scientific method Paul Ivanovich uses later in "Gusev." But Vasilyev is "keenly and splendidly sensitive" to other people's pain, responding to it in a manner similar to Ivan in "Ward Number Six." His rational approach doesn't help and Vasilyev slides further into spiritual anguish and begins to contemplate suicide. In portraying Vasilyev's altered state of mind, Chekhov felt he had "described mental pain correctly, and in conformity with all the canons of psychiatry" (IV, 265). At this point, Vasilyev seeks medical help. As happens so often in Chekhov's work, the virtuous doctor figure appears. Vasilyev confronts this doctor with the question that induced his struggle: "Is prostitution an evil or isn't it?" (IV, 178). When the doctor replies unequivocally that it is, Vasilyev feels "an immense pity" for all mankind, and then begins to recover. His subjective view of the nature of man has been reaffirmed by the doctor. In contrast to Ivan in "Ward Number Six," who remains hospitalized as a paranoid, Vasilyev resolves his disabling conflict.

That conflict between a subjective view of the world and objective reality takes a different, Gothic turn in "The Black Monk" (Hingley). In this moral allegory, the protagonist who experiences that conflict is another of Chekhov's scientist doctors, a distinguished scholar and lecturer in psychology who studies general philosophy. Like the doctor in "An Awkward Business," Kovrin suffers from overwork and emotional exhaustion and seeks rest at the estate of his foster father, who has a daughter named Tanya. Out in the country, Kovrin plunges back into work, but on a walk one evening, he is visited by a legendary apparition called the Black Monk. The figure moves at awesome speed like a whirlwind over the fields, pausing to wink at Kovrin before he disappears into thin air. Although inspired by the experience, Kovrin concludes it is an hallucination, and keeps it to himself as he discusses the future of mankind with Tanya's father, and begins to fall in love with Tanya.

When the Black Monk reappears, Kovrin engages the figure in a conversation about the future of mankind. The Monk says Kovrin is one of the "Elect," dedicated to the "Rational and the Beautiful," who will lead mankind toward a "great and glorious" future. This dialogue recalls the moral allegories of Nathaniel Hawthorne (1804–1864). Like the figure of the devil in the Hawthorne story, "Young Goodman Brown" (1835), the Black Monk may be a hallucination, the production of an altered mind or an actual presence. The Monk tells Kovrin he is ill because he is overworked: "You've worn yourself out. You have sacrificed your health to the Ideal, in other words, and ere long you'll sacrifice your very life to it" (VII, 90). Once again, the situation recalls a Hawthorne story, "The Birthmark" (1846), in which the scientist doctor Aylmer sacrifices his wife, and his happiness, to the Ideal, the Rational, and the Beautiful. Like Aylmer and like the doctor in "An Awkward Business," Kovrin is a man who has sacrificed his youth, strength, and mental health for his work.

The struggle between Kovrin's subjective world and his objective, social reality causes Kovrin to experience a mental breakdown. However, in the process, he gains a vision of a "lofty" and "beatific" destiny for himself. The question remains whether this vision is finally a real or appropriate one, or whether it is simply a result of excess. This ambiguity is lacking in most Gothic narratives, which focus simply on creating terror in the reader.

In contrast to Vasilyev in "A Nervous Breakdown," Kovrin never satisfactorily integrates his subjective view of the world into the objective, social reality. Eventually, he dies from a hemorrhage. Kovrin is certainly not as sympathetic a character as Vasilyev. Hawthorne's comments on Aylmer could as well apply to Kovrin: had he "reached a profounder wisdom, he need not have flung away the happiness which would have woven his mortal life to the selfsame texture with the celestial." Kovrin is like Aylmer in that the "momentary circumstance was too strong for him; he failed to look beyond the shadowy scope of time, and, living once for all in eternity, to find the perfect future in the present" ("The Birthmark").

Stories of the Peasant

In contrast to the uplifting spiritual experiences of the two peasant women in "The Student," the experiences of the peasant characters in other stories from this period are brutal and without a positive spiritual dimension. Chekhov's affinities with the movement of Naturalism appear in "Thieves" and "Peasant Women." In both stories, the monotonous, unfulfilled lives of the protagonists lead them to desire a freedom that they feel is attainable only through criminal acts. In these stories, Chekhov explores the tension between the needs and desires of the individual and the requirements of the community and its laws.

In "Thieves" (Hingley), the protagonist, a medical orderly named Yergunov, has an experience one night that alters the course of his life: during a violent snowstorm he seeks shelter at an isolated inn where he encounters a notorious horse thief who later steals his horse. But the next morning, instead of being angry at the theft, Yergunov begins to question the everyday life which most men lead. His own gray, monotonous existence, his wages, and his subordinate position seem "contemptible and sickening" to him now (V, 99). As the story closes eighteen months later, Yergunov learns the thief has cut the innkeeper's throat and robbed her, and Yergunov envies the thief. Now Yergunov seeks some rich man's house to burgle; he, too, will become a criminal.

The story's objective presentation of these events caused the editor who printed the story to accuse Chekhov of indifference to good and evil. This accusation prompted Chekhov to reply that juries should decide on the guilt of horse thieves, for "my business is only to show them as they are"; he believed it would be nice "to couple art with sermonizing" but that "personally, I find this exceedingly difficult, and, because of conditions imposed by technique, all but impossible" (Yarmolinsky, 133). These technical considerations are the basis of Chekhov's narrative art. He declares: "When I write, I rely fully on the reader, on the assumption that he himself will add the subjective elements that are lacking in the story" (Yarmolinsky, 133). In "Thieves," these "subjective elements" posit a community's laws and the desires of the individual. As an artist, Chekhov attempts not to resolve that tension, but to portray it objectively.

In "Peasant Women" (Hingley), published a year after "Thieves," two women desire to escape their lives of hardship and boredom. Barbara and Sophia live with their father-in-law, a local merchant who runs a tavern and lodges travellers overnight. After Sophia's husband became foreman of a factory and took up with another woman, he sent Sophia home to live with his father. Barbara is married to the younger son, a drunken hunchback she detests and married only because of her poverty, but now feels like a slave, as if she were "caught like a rat in a trap" (V, 126), and would rather "sleep with a viper" than with her husband.

The dramatic action begins when a businessman stops for the night, and tells a long story about his liaison with his neighbor's wife, who was eventually convicted of poisoning her husband. This story gives rise to Barbara's talk later that night with Sophia. Barbara confesses she is having an affair with the local cleric's son, and declares she would rather be an old maid, go begging, or even throw herself headfirst down a well, than live as she does. Both women work "like horses" and never hear a "kind word." As the singing of Barbara's lover drifts to them in the night, Sophia feels a "whiff of freedom" and envies Barbara, as Yergunov envied the horse thief. Barbara declares she could kill her husband and "think nothing of it," and proposes that she and Sophia kill both her husband and their father-in-law. But after discussing the idea, Barbara tells Sophia to dismiss it, and the story closes with the businessman leaving the next morning. The suggestion of violence remains just a suggestion, revealing the limited, stark lives of these women. The naturalistic details of Chekhov's portrayal of the latent brutality in peasant life look forward to his later novellas, "Peasants" and "In the Hollow," in which that violence is dramatically realized.

The Master, 1895–1903

Raymond Carver believed an agreement might be reached among "thoughtful" readers that Chekhov was the greatest short story writer who ever lived, not only because of the "immense number" of stories he wrote, but the "awesome frequency" with which he produced masterpieces.[41] That frequency is most apparent in this last period, from 1895 through 1903, when Chekhov treated the same subjects, but with a shift in point of view technique to include a narrating author persona in many stories. In general, this persona is disembodied, commenting on the characters and action as do the narrators in Henry James and George Eliot. A. P. Chudakov remarks that his characteristic manner of "depicting the world through a *concrete, perceiving consciousness*" has not been replaced. Rather the "old manner remains and a new one is added to it" (99–100).

Chekhov's contemporaries noticed this shift in point of view. One critic commented in 1898 that Chekhov was no longer the "objective artist" he had been earlier; that same year, another critic perceived that Chekhov's "added subjectivity" would deepen the content of his creative work (Chudakov, 73). The modern critic Nicholas Moravcevich traces the evolution of Chekhov's earlier artistic creed of strict objectivity to the new "persuasiveness" of his "artistic aims," a transformation that gradually occurred over a five-year span from 1887 to 1892; Moravcevich believes this different approach marked the end of Chekhov's formative period and the beginning of his "transcendence of the aesthetic dictates of naturalism" (225).

Stories of Love and the Authentic Life

"A Lady with a Dog" (Hingley) beautifully illustrates Chekhov's use of a shift in point of view, for in addition to the perceiving consciousness of the protagonist, comment is presented directly to the reader through Chekhov's disembodied narrating persona. Like many of Chekhov's middle-class protagonists, the bank employee Gurov does not have a satisfactory relationship with his wife. He fears her because she is outspoken and intellectual. Any happiness he finds with women occurs in a series of affairs, and while on vacation in Yalta, he engages in what appears to be another such affair. The woman, the "lady with the dog," is named Anne, and on an outing to a church at Oreanda, the couple sit on a bench, entranced by the view. Shifting beyond Gurov's conscious mind, Chekhov adopts a narrating persona who relates that "borne up from below, the sea's monotonous, muffled boom spoke of peace, of the everlasting sleep awaiting us" (IX, 132). This passage has a mystical dimension that recalls the last section of "Gusev," also narrated beyond the conscious mind of the protagonist. The comment becomes more lyrical as it develops in a passage on eternity and the indifference of the universe, which measures not only Gurov but the reader against its endless vastness. It concludes with an optimistic comment on the eternal nature of life—not on the individual, who is mortal, but on life itself which is immortal and constantly progressing, a recurring motif in Chekhov's stories from this period.

The paragraph closes with a return to Gurov's mind as he reflects that "everything on earth is beautiful, really, when you consider it— everything but what we think and do ourselves when we forget the lofty goals of being and our human dignity" (IX, 132). This thought, mirroring Chekhov's own sensibilities, makes Gurov a more sympathetic character. Although he lives an inauthentic life—in which he speaks disparagingly of women, calling them the "inferior species"—he is capable of this insightful observation when sitting beside Anne. The couple takes a number of excursions which invariably leave an impression of "majesty and beauty," while a subtle transformation begins to occur in each of them. Anne articulates her desire for that transformation when she voices her yearning for a different life—in Chekhov, such a desire is usually the telltale sign of a character's living an inauthentic life. Like Gurov, she does not love her spouse, but her adulterous relationship with Gurov disturbs her because she wants to live a "decent, moral life."

Gurov on the other hand easily dismisses the affair until he returns to his inauthentic life in Moscow. There he resumes his boring life of "futile activities," realizing such meaningless activities "engross most of your time, your best efforts, and you end up with a sort of botched, pedestrian life: a form of imbecility from which there's no way out, no escape" (IX, 135). Gurov's thought recalls the final comments of Nikitin on his domestic life in "The Russian Master": "You might as well be in jail or in a madhouse" (IX, 135). Gurov feels the same desperation Anne felt before her vacation in Yalta, a desperation marked by the feeling she could not control herself. He now flees Moscow to seek out Anne, because their affair has become the most important aspect of his life. This transformation in Gurov's attitude constitutes the dramatic climax of the plot.

After Gurov finds Anne, their situation develops into a prolonged affair, and Gurov begins to live two lives. One is the false life he has been living, full of "stereotyped truths and stereotyped untruth," identical to the life of his friends and acquaintances. He despises this inauthentic life, and feels that "everything vital, interesting and crucial to him, everything which called his sincerity and integrity into play, everything which made up the core of his life" (IX, 139) occurs in his other, secret life with Anne. In contrast to those protagonists from earlier stories such as "Lights" and "The Duel" who undergo a transformation and throw off their inauthentic lives, Gurov retains his old life in the form of a facade that satisfies the decorum of the age. This compromise makes him a more complex character, a typical modern hero unable to integrate his multiple lives into one.

As the story closes, both Anne and he feel their love has "transformed" them, but the most difficult part of their lives is "only just beginning" (IX, 141). Chekhov's method of ending a story with the suggestion that the lives of his characters will go on developing becomes one of his most effective closures during this period. This conclusion reinforces the theme that through love—one of Chekhov's favorite topics—the characters have been transformed, making them better people.

Chekhov approaches the power of love with a different tone, achieved partially through a shift in point of view, in "Angel" (Hingley). Chekhov has a tongue-in-cheek attitude toward the protagonist, Olga, who is "always in love with someone—couldn't help it" (IX, 82). She is a "quiet, good-hearted, sentimental, very healthy young lady with a tender, melting expression" (IX, 82) to whom men are attracted and to whom women respond openly and kindly. At first Chekhov conveys his criticism through light satire as Olga marries a theater manager and adopts his opinions in all matters, especially on the importance of the theater. When the theater manager dies a few years later, she marries a lumberyard manager and in turn adopts his opinions in all matters, including the idea that the theater is a "trifle." Olga is not consciously insincere, merely naive and shallow.

When the lumberyard manager dies after six years—during which the couple prayed for children but had none—Olga falls in love with an army veterinarian who is estranged from his wife, and, in turn, takes up his opinions. But when he is transferred, Olga goes through a crisis because "she no longer had views on anything"—she cannot form her own opinions. She feels she needs a love "to possess her whole being, all her mind and soul: a love to equip her with ideas, with a sense of purpose, a love to warm her ageing blood" (IX, 88). This function of love is the object of Chekhov's satire. Although Chekhov presents some of Olga's experiences from her perspective, he also addresses much of the action directly to the reader. In earlier works, "Ward Number Six" and "Three Years," for example, the passages outside the consciousness of the characters are almost always pure exposition, unmediated by the assertive voice of a separate, vital narrating persona.

To this point in the action, "Angel" satirizes Olga's sensibility in an amusing series of events without a focused form, reading more like a character sketch than a story. What makes the work a masterpiece is the last episode, in which the tone shifts to one of compassion for the protagonist, much as it does for Jacob in "Rothschild's Fiddle." With this shift, the character is redeemed in the reader's eye, becoming worthy of respect and sympathy. After a half-dozen years, the veterinarian returns as a civilian with his wife and son, and Olga emotionally adopts the child, a nine-year-old boy named Sasha. Olga cares for all his needs as her love for him becomes boundless, eclipsing her earlier loves. Olga's desire to love, which Chekhov has been satirizing, now becomes meaningful by its very compassion: "For this boy—no relative at all—for his dimpled cheeks, for his cap she would give her whole life, give it gladly, with tears of ecstasy. Why? Who knows?" The satire is absent from this statement, which is as straightforward as the closing passage of "A Lady with a Dog." The question "Why? Who knows?"—Chekhov directly addressing the reader—deftly deepens the reader's involvement in the action.

"Angel" has generated a number of widely different critical interpretations. One of the more insightful comes from an anonymous reviewer in 1916 who notes Chekhov possessed the "subtlest sympathy," which enables him to "understand and reveal" his characters; this critic maintains that the effect of reading Chekhov's tales is to be "washed free of petty impatience and acerbity of judgement."[42]

In "Ariadne" (Hingley), the character of Olga in "The Butterfly" is recast into a colder, more calculating young woman, and in place of the virtuous Dr. Dymov is a sensitive, idealistic young landowner,

Shamokhin, who must resolve his feelings for the woman who makes him a victim of his love. Dr. Dymov escapes his situation with Olga through death, but in this later story, Chekhov develops the situation to its more complex, more logical, and more realistic conclusion.

Shamokhin narrates his story to a first-person character. As in the earlier stories, "Easter Eve" and "Uprooted," this first-person character is a writer. The difference between this character and the persona identified in "A Lady with a Dog" and "Angel" is that in "Ariadne" the narrator is an actual character who interacts with another character, Shamokhin, not simply a narrating voice. The setting of the frame of "Ariadne" provides a backdrop for the telling of Shamokhin's story: the two men are on the passenger deck of a Black Sea steamer when Shamokhin makes some general comments on the nature of women and love, comments that recall the initial attitude of Gurov in "A Lady with a Dog": because of disappointing love affairs, he looks upon women as "mean, restless, lying, unfair, primitive, cruel creatures" (VIII, 74). Shamokhin then relates his specific story to illustrate this opinion.

A few years previously, in his mid twenties, Shamokhin fell very much in love with a neighbor's sister, Ariadne, a beautiful woman whose selfish demands for luxurious items were bringing her brother's estate to ruin. Like many of Chekhov's landowners, Shamokhin is an idealist who "romanticizes" love, but he is wise enough to realize Ariadne is so self-centered, so taken with her own beauty and charm, that she is incapable of really loving another person. However, Shamokhin cannot resist her, so he follows her to Europe and eventually becomes her lover. There they live at resorts with the money Shamokhin obtains from his father, who must mortgage their estate to pay for the extravagance. Like Olga in "The Butterfly," Ariadne begins painting, but her real interest is "to attract": she must "bewitch, captivate, drive people out of their minds" (VIII, 90). Although Ariadne is without much taste, she is "diabolically sharp and cunning, and in company she had the knack of passing as educated and progressive" (VIII, 91). She is one of Chekhov's least likeable characters, a hypocrite whose behavior causes some critics to condemn her, and others to find in her an attack upon the marriage customs and lack of opportunities for women of the day.

After a short while, Shamokhin falls out of love and yearns to return to Russia, "to work and earn my bread by the sweat of my brow and make good my mistakes" (VIII, 92). This desire is a common goal for Chekhov's idealistic heroes—the same salvation through work the engineer espouses in "Lights" and Vanya clings to in the play *Uncle Vanya*. The story closes with a return to the frame, where the author character argues against Shamokhin's attitude toward women, maintaining one cannot generalize from Ariadne on the nature of women, but Shamokhin remains unconvinced. In contrast to Olga and Dymov in "The Butterfly," the relationship between Shamokhin and Ariadne is portrayed over the entire course of its development and decline in a remarkable illustration of Chekhov's mastery of point-of-view technique.

The situation of a person trapped in a frustrating, harmful relationship is also the subject of "The Order of St. Anne" (Hingley). The narrative is often at a considerable distance from the heroine, but at times, shifts into her mind. In contrast to Ariadne, the young woman is a sympathetic character, and her husband takes advantage of her. Chekhov begins the story outside the consciousness of the heroine, commenting on people's response to a government official of fifty-two marrying an eighteen-year-old girl. Anne, the daughter of a recent widower, marries the wealthy official for independence and security, hoping to help her family, but in Chekhov, marrying for such reasons is inviting trouble.

Once married, Anne realizes she doesn't even like Modeste, her husband, and soon discovers she now has less money than before since Modeste will give her nothing. But, afraid to protest, she forces herself "to smile and pretend to be pleased when defiled by clumsy caresses and embraces that sickened her" (VIII, 36). Anne's position suddenly changes, however, when Modeste has her attend a ball to impress his supervisor and colleagues, where she dazzles the dignitaries in Cinderella-like fashion. The next day, after Modeste's supervisor visits the house to thank her for her attendance, Modeste appears before her with the "crawling, sugary, slavish, deferential look" (VIII, 41) he keeps for powerful people. With her newly won power, Anne now gains the upper hand, and begins spending his money freely, cavorting with other men in an ironic reversal of her situation: she is now the one who orders Modeste about. However, Modeste is not dissatisfied, for he receives a medal—the Order of St. Anne, Second Class—from his supervisor. Ronald Hingley observes that this story is one of the many by Chekhov that are only a "mere dozen pages" but seem to have the content of full-length novels because of Chekhov's ability to "conjure up a whole milieu by suggestion without needing to fill in every detail" (VIII, 7). The government official's desiring the medal, his fawning before a superior, and the ironic reversal recall Chekhov's early humorous period.

In contrast to the coarse, philistine Modeste is the idealistic, sensitive artist in "The Artist's Story" (Hingley). A landscape painter, his idealism resembles that of Shamokhin in "Ariadne." In commenting on first-person stories from this period, A. P. Chudakov notes a shift in narrative technique away from the "individualized features" of the protagonist's speech toward a conventional literary narrator, similar to the use of the persona in such third-person stories as "A Lady with a Dog," "Angel," and "The Order of St. Anne." (69). In both instances, strict objectivity is replaced by the author's presence. Because the pretext in "Ariadne" is that the author himself is a character, the conventional literary narration is justified; but in "An Artist's Story," the narrative suggests a written manuscript although the story mentions none. Like Shamokhin, the narrator—he remains unnamed in the story—falls in love with a young woman from a neighboring estate, but unlike Ariadne, this girl, Zhenya, is sensitive and caring. Only seventeen or eighteen, Zhenya is five years younger than her sister, Lydia, who dominates the family, even their mother.

Lydia is an idealist, like the narrator, but her ideals have led her in a different, more practical direction: she builds schools and hospitals for the local peasants and teaches them herself. The artist, on the other hand, believes such efforts actually are keeping the peasants in poverty. He maintains a radical transformation of society is required for any real change. In one of the arguments between the narrator and Lydia, he declares that the peasants must be freed from their manual labor so that they can develop meaningful, spiritual lives. Otherwise, he believes work has no meaning, and thus refuses to do any. Lydia rejects his position, accusing him of simply saying "charming things" to excuse his laziness, for she believes "rejecting hospitals and schools is easier than healing or teaching" (VIII, 108). She believes such work is more valuable than "all the landscapes ever painted" (VIII, 109). This exchange of ideas is effective as fiction because Chekhov is portraying characters whose ideas are an integral part of their individuality.

But the artist finally is no match for Lydia with her practical sense. Lydia forbids Zhenya to ever see the narrator again, ordering Zhenya and her mother to leave the district. The story closes as the narrator relates that several years after his departure from the district he learned that Lydia continues to teach, struggling to improve the life of the peasants, and Zhenya no longer lives in the district. Now when he paints, he recalls their love, and it seems to him as if soon they shall meet again. Chekhov poignantly evokes a sense of expectation in the character that the reader is aware can never be realized.

The complexity of the story evolves from the ambiguity of the characters' situations. The narrator and Zhenya are both sensitive and sympathetic, and their love is obviously a beautiful, desirable emotion. The hard-working idealist Lydia, although a valuable member of her community, is the very person who makes the further development of that love impossible. Once again, Chekhov presents no solutions to his characters' problems in life.

Love is the subject of another landowner's story in "Concerning Love" (Hingley), which shares characters and a narrative approach with "A Hard Case" and "Gooseberries." Because of these similarities, critics refer to these stories as the "Little Trilogy." One function of the frame setting for the story—the opening and closing sections are in the third person—is to set the atmosphere for the landowner's inner story. Two sportsmen—Ivan Ivanovich, a veterinarian, and Burkin, a teacher—have been caught in a rainstorm while out hunting, so they must spend the night at the estate of Alyokhin, a landowner. The next day at lunch, Alyokhin comments on the general "mystery" of love in a metaphor that is not only particularly appropriate for Chekhov as a doctor, but can be applied to his poetics in short fiction: "What seems to fit one instance doesn't fit a dozen others. It's best to interpret each instance separately in my view, without trying to generalize. We must isolate each individual case, as doctors say" (IX, 41). The comparison to a case history is an apt one for many of Chekhov's stories, and Alyokhin's further comment on a lack of a solution in love suggests Chekhov's own position.

In Alyokhin's particular case, he took up farming his estate—"not without a certain repugnance"—to pay off the mortgage, and over the course of several years, he and a married woman who lived in town fell in love. However, because of her family duties, and because of Alyokhin's sense of responsibility to her household, they did not declare their love to each other. She eventually became depressed, feeling that her life was unfulfilled and wasted. When her husband secures a judgeship in a different province, the family moves away. As they part for the last time, Alyokhin realizes how inessential, how trivial, and how deceptive and unnecessary everything that frustrated their love was. As the story closes, the narrating persona returns to comment on how the two listeners—Ivan and Burkin—feel compassion for Alyokhin, and regret he has nothing to make his life more pleasant. This sense of regret, of love unfulfilled, of wasted opportunities and unlived lives, is the essence of the popular Chekhovian mood.

Stories of the Authentic Life

These aspects of the Chekhovian mood also are present in another story published in 1898, "All Friends Together" (Hingley). The structure does not resemble "Concerning Love" as much as a more complex "Verotchka," published eleven years earlier in 1887. As in "Verotchka," a professional man from the city travels to the provinces where he has the opportunity for a life of love, but like the protagonist in "Verotchka," he rejects that opportunity. The story is filtered through the consciousness of Podgorin, a successful lawyer who visits the estate of some old friends, where he had served as a tutor when a poor student. Both the types of characters and the estate's atmosphere resemble the characters and setting of Chekhov's later plays: because of mismanagement, the estate is to be sold, as in *The Cherry Orchard*; and the three women and Sergy are similar in many ways to the family in *The Three Sisters*. The story should not be confused with the earlier prose plays where the structure is composed of dialogue, for the interior, psychological action in Podgorin's consciousness is the structural center of this story.

The dramatic line of development involves Podgorin's relationship with Nadya. Ten years before, Podgorin had tutored her, and later, fallen in love with her. Now Nadya, an attractive, twenty-three-year-old, desires to marry, and the plot revolves around whether Podgorin will propose. One moonlit summer night, when Podgorin is sitting out on the grounds, Nadya appears. She senses his presence, but since she cannot see him in the shadows, she asks if someone is there. Podgorin knows that now is the time to speak, if he wishes to propose, but like the protagonist in "Verotchka," he feels strangely indifferent. His emotions remain disengaged from this "poetic vision" of the woman in the moonlight. Podgorin remains silent, and Nadya turns away with the comment, "There's no one there" (IX, 242). On one level, her "no one" suggests Podgorin's lack of substance as a human being, for he has rejected the opportunity to become part of this "poetic vision," the chance for a life of love. In his action, Podgorin on a deeper level rejects himself: "this Podgorin with his apathy, his boredom, his perpetual bad temper, his inability to adapt to real life" (IX, 241). Shortly afterward, Podgorin leaves for Moscow, feeling "indifferent," not sad.

In "Verotchka," the protagonist's rejection is a clear-cut turning away from a vital, life experience, but Podgorin's choice is more ambiguous. He does not wish to become entangled in the web of problems in Nadya's family, and more importantly, he yearns for a "new, lofty, rational mode of existence" (IX, 241), which he senses this marriage could not provide. The desire to change one's life is a common trait of the Chekhov protagonist who senses he is living an inauthentic life.

A story published later in 1898, "Dr. Startsev" (Hingley), is similar to "All Friends Together" in subject, but where "All Friends Together" has the tight dramatic focus of a play, "Dr. Startsev" suggests a novel that has been marvelously telescoped into a short story. Instead of the highly focused time span of one day, which leads itself to remaining exclusively in the consciousness of the protagonist, the time in "Dr. Startsev" spans several years, during which the protagonist ages considerably and his position in society changes. The story provides a good example of Chekhov's narrating persona, with several shifts into the consciousness of the protagonist during key dramatic moments.

In the opening, the narrator provides a general introduction to a provincial town and to the Turkins, the town's most cultivated and accomplished family. Dr. Startsev, a young doctor recently appointed to the area, falls in love with an aspiring pianist named Catherine Turkin, but when he proposes, Catherine rejects him. Although she believes he is kind and intelligent, she is determined to escape the provincial town with its "empty, futile existence" (IX, 60). In the four years that pass after Catherine leaves for Moscow, Startsev settles into a middle-class existence: he grows to resent the limited views of the provincial towns-people, gains a great amount of weight, and becomes a nightly bridge player. When Catherine returns after her discovery that she will never become a great pianist, she desires Startsev's company, but he rejects her request to call upon her.

The story closes after a few more years in which Startsev has built a vast practice, and has gained even more weight. Now a dedicated materialist primarily interested in acquiring property, he lives a dreary life without other interests. Like Podgorin, he has rejected the opportunity for a different life, and the narrator describes him as a rather pathetic figure. In commenting on the artistic merit of the story, Ronald Hingley observes that although "Dr. Startsev" has been comparatively neglected by the critics, the story holds its own with any rival (IX, 1).

Life in the provinces takes a different turn in "The Savage" (Hingley), in which the protagonist is not Chekhov's typical middle-class hero but an elderly, retired Cossack officer who invites a lawyer to his farm. At the farmhouse, the lawyer discovers the Cossack's wife is still young and pretty, although the couple has two full-grown sons. But the Cossack treats her with indifference: "She wasn't a wife, she wasn't the mistress of the house or even a servant, she was more of a dependent—an unwanted poor relation, a nobody" (VIII, 232). This deplorable condition is dramatized not only by the manner in which the Cossack orders his wife about, but when the Cossack says that "women aren't really human to my way of thinking" (VIII, 231).

The Cossack's treatment of his wife is but one form of his behavior that the lawyer finds objectionable, and Chekhov's achievement in the story is in portraying this very unsympathetic character in human terms. Because of a recent stroke, the Cossack is searching for "something to hold on to in his old age," some belief so he will not be afraid of dying. For all his callous behavior, the old Cossack knows that for the "good of his soul" he should shake off "the laziness" that causes "day after day and year after year to be engulfed unnoticed, leaving no trace" (VIII, 232). Despite his cultural difference, the Cossack displays the same search for individual meaning exhibited by Chekhov's common middle-class protagonists.

Another character like Dr. Startsev who becomes confined to a life in the provinces is the heroine of "Home" (Hingley). Vera, a sensitive, educated, young woman, returns to her grandfather's farm after ten years in Moscow. At first, she is excited about her life in the country, although the wide-open landscape with its "boundless plain" is "so monotonous, so empty" it frightens her, and although she has reservations about her grandfather, who before emancipation had his peasants flogged and who still terrorizes his servants. But as Vera discovers the limited nature of the provincial society—she had never met people so "casual and indifferent"—her feelings about her life and future begin to change to uncertainty, and like so many Chekhov characters, she yearns for something to give her life meaning, a situation which will enable her to "love and have a family of her own" (VIII, 244).

Vera's aunt suggests that Vera marry Dr. Neshchapov, who is attracted to Vera. In his materialism, this doctor shares characteristics with Dr. Startsev: the director of a factory, he considers his medical practice his secondary profession. Vera is not attracted to him, but her other possibilities seem even more limiting, for the "vast expanses, the long winters, the monotony and tedium make you feel so helpless" (VIII, 246). She fears that disabling boredom so many Chekhov protagonists experience, but "there seemed to be no way out. Why do anything when nothing does any good?" (VIII, 246). One day Vera vents her frustration on her servant. Realizing the inappropriateness of her action—she detests such behavior in her grandfather—she agrees to marry Dr. Neshchapov, and thus resigns herself to her own "perpetual discontent with herself and others" (VIII, 247), the same discontent that Podgorin displays. Defeated, she accepts that "happiness and truth have nothing to do with ordinary life" (VIII, 247). In surrendering her aspirations and dreams for a better life, Vera knows she will now "expect nothing better." The provincial social reality will overcome her desire for a better, richer life.

Chekhov had a special place in his heart for schoolteachers, and it shows in "In the Cart" (Hingley), published five weeks after "Home" in 1897. The events are structured around the journey of a rural schoolmistress. As in "All Friends Together" and "Home," the story is centered in the consciousness of the protagonist, Marya, who has taught at the same school for thirteen years, although to her, the constant hardship makes it seem a "hundred years or more." During Marya's journey, a local landowner, an alcoholic about her age, passes Marya's cart in his carriage. She feels attracted to him, but knows to fall in love would be a "disaster." Although she desires a husband and wants "love and happiness," she feels her job has made her unattractive, and so her love would not be returned.

Through her thoughts, Chekhov details the hardships of her position. All winter she must endure the cold schoolhouse, and she must struggle constantly against the attitudes of the janitor and the school manager. She realizes that no one finds her attractive, for the job is wearing her out, making her a drudge ashamed of her timid behavior. Her salary is low, and she is so worried about finances that she misses the satisfaction of serving an ideal in her work.

As Marya enters her home village, she sees a woman on a train who resembles her dead mother, reminding Marya of her life before teaching. This experience gives her a sudden surge of happiness and joy, a form of rapture. When the landowner again appears, she imagines "such happiness as has never been on earth" (VIII, 258). She feels the sky and trees and building windows are "aglow with her triumphant happiness" (VIII, 258). This mystical experience, which resembles the happiness of Gusev, is the climax of the story.

But this wonderful experience vanishes as Marya's cart continues into the village, leaving her "shivering, numb with cold." She realizes she will continue her joyless life as before. She is trapped as firmly in her barren, provincial environment as Vera or Dr. Startsev. In commenting on her character, however, Kenneth Lantz notes that she is not "fixed, limited, easily defined," but a character in flux: he compares her to

Nadya Shimin in "A Marriageable Girl," contending that characters such as these are "alive"—they are "unpredictable, and they can develop."[43]

In many ways "A Marriageable Girl" (Hingley), the last short story Chekhov wrote, stands in opposition to such stories as "Dr. Startsev," "Home," and "In the Cart." Unlike Vera, who decides that marriage is the only available option, or Marya, who desires the opportunity for a suitor, the protagonist Nadya escapes her inauthentic life by a brave decision. When the story opens, Nadya has a fiancé whom she will marry in a few weeks, but she becomes depressed. Nadya attempts to tell her mother about this depression, but her widowed mother does not understand. A friend of the family, Sasha, encourages Nadya to flee the engagement and her home. He is one of those revolutionary students in Chekhov who advocates radical change—Trofimov in *The Cherry Orchard*, written immediately after "A Marriageable Girl," is another example. Sasha accuses the whole family, including Nadya, of being "sordid and immoral" in their idleness. Although Nadya agrees with Sasha's criticism, she feels trapped in her situation and unable to change it.

A critical point comes a few weeks before the marriage, when her fiancé takes her to inspect their luxurious future house. Nadya hates it. She realizes she also hates her fiancé's "sheer complacency," and "sheer stupid, mindless, intolerable smugness" (IX, 214–15). Afterwards Nadya explains to her mother that she cannot marry the man, and declares that their lives are "petty and degrading" and that she despises herself and "this idle, pointless existence" (IX, 217). In contrast to Vera in "Home," Nadya does not submit to the objective, social reality of her circumstances, but begins a transformation of her life that affirms her subjective view of the world. The next day she runs away to St. Petersburg to go to school, "on her way to freedom." Ronald Hingley notes that in the story's own time, Nadya would have been readily identified as a revolutionary figure (IX, 10); she feels a "new life opening before her, with its broad horizons" (IX, 223). In contrast to Vera in "Home," Nadya does not settle for a life she knows will eventually defeat her. The last of Chekhov's great fiction protagonists, Nadya is a heroine in a most positive manner, a final tribute to Chekhov's ability to view each story as a fresh effort in his search for artistic integrity.

If the character of Nadya represents a challenge to the restrictions imposed by society, then Belikov, the protagonist of "A Hard Case" (Hingley), represents the other extreme. Belikov demands that everyone rigidly conform to the restrictions and rules of the objective, social reality. Like the others in the informal trilogy, "Concerning Love" and "Gooseberries," there is a story within a story. Burkin, a schoolteacher, relates the inner story of Belikov to Ivan, the veterinarian surgeon, in a village barn after a day of hunting. Belikov, who died a few months before, was a classics teacher who had taught at the local school for fifteen years. He had terrorized not only other schoolteachers and students, but the whole town with his strict adherence to the rules. Out of fear of Belikov's disapproval, the townspeople gave up their amateur theatricals, and the clergy would not eat meat or play cards in his presence. Instead of directly bullying the townspeople like Sergeant Prishibeyev, Belikov, also one of Chekhov's more famous characters, intimidates them with the authority of his position.

Chekhov's portrayal of Belikov's personal life gives the character credibility. Belikov was afraid of life: he feared "repercussions" in his job, feared his throat would be cut by his servant, feared burglars; and the crowded school itself "terrified him, revolted his whole being" (IX, 18). Belikov's undoing begins when a Ukrainian woman moves to town, and the townspeople decide the two of them should marry. When Belikov sees the Ukrainian woman riding a bicycle, he goes to her brother to protest what he feels is a lack of decorum. But the brother—a robust, new teacher—tosses Belikov out of his lodgings, and he falls down the stairs. Although he is unhurt, the Ukrainian woman and some other ladies laugh at his ludicrous expression. Greatly upset, Belikov returns home where he goes to bed for a month, until he dies. Burkin remembers that after the funeral everyone enjoyed an hour or two of "absolute freedom," but within a week, life was back to its "old rut. It was just as austere, wearisome, and pointless as before" (IX, 25).

Burkin closes his inner story with the comment that Belikov left behind a lot of other men in "shells" who will continue to be a force in the future. In contrast to Nadya from "A Marriageable Girl," such men have a fixed response to life, and in their rigidity are living inauthentic lives, incapable of change or growth. Ivan believes everyone in the provincial town is living in a "shell," like Belikov, and expresses the desire to tell an "extremely edifying" story himself, but since Burkin is tired and soon falls asleep, Ivan is left pondering the story he wanted to tell. On one level, this ending is an effective closure to the story, for Burkin's story strikes a moral chord in Ivan that makes him want to relate his own tale. On another level, it sets the stage for the next story in the trilogy.

Ivan relates his "edifying" story, "Gooseberries" (Hingley), on another hunting trip. Again Chekhov uses his narrator persona to establish the frame setting for Ivan's story: it begins raining, so the two men seek shelter on the estate of Alyokhin, who later will narrate "Concerning Love," the last story in the trilogy. Over tea, Ivan begins his tale of his brother Nicholas, who spent much of his life saving for a small estate like the one on which the brothers spent their childhood. The dramatic section of Ivan's inner story occurs a year before his present narration, when he first visited Nicholas' estate. Nicholas, like Dr. Startsev, had gained weight; in describing him, his dog, and his cook, Ivan employs imagery that recalls pigs, so that Nicholas himself seems "all set to grunt." Nicholas has undergone a great change, and behaves like "a real squire, a man of property." Ivan believes he has become blatantly arrogant, with a typical landowner's attitude toward his peasants; he believes education is not right for "the lower orders," and corporal punishment is "in certain cases useful and indispensible" (IX, 34).

The important change in the story, however, occurs in Ivan himself, which is appropriate since he is the point-of-view character. During the long years of saving, Nicholas dreamed of eating gooseberries from his estate, and his first action as owner was to order twenty bushes and plant them himself. A few hours after Ivan's arrival, when Nicholas picks his first gooseberries and, in silence and tears, eats them, Ivan realizes Nicholas is a happy man. But that realization plunges Ivan into a "despondency akin to despair." Later that night Ivan realizes what a crushing force the happy people of the world are, for among the "grotesque poverty everywhere, the overcrowding, degeneracy, drunkenness and hypocrisy" (IX, 35), there is the impudence and idleness of the strong. Ivan believes happy people have "no eyes or ears" for those who suffer, and the "silent happiness" of a community is a collective hypnosis that allows such suffering to continue simply as "mute statistics" (IX, 35–36). Because of this system, Ivan believes at the door of every contented man should be someone standing with a little hammer, someone to keep "dinning into his head" that unhappy people do exist, and that, happy though he may be, life "will round on him sooner or later" (IX, 36).

In presenting this idea, Ivan becomes a voice advocating a moral position that underlies much of Chekhov's work in the last decade of his life, from the character of the earlier Ivan in "Ward Number Six" in 1892 to the revolutionary Sasha in "A Marriageable Girl" in 1903. In "Gooseberries," Ivan relates this realization has worked a change in him, a kind of moral conversion, so now he finds the peace and quiet of town life unbearable, and no spectacle more depressing than a happy family having tea around a table. Ivan's search for meaning and authenticity in life becomes the focus for the larger moral content of the story.

When the story returns to the frame setting, the dissatisfaction of the listeners with Ivan's story is portrayed with Chekhov's tongue-in-cheek tone as they wish for a different kind of story, one about elegant persons that does not bore them. With this comment, Chekhov makes a light, ironic statement about the stereotypical concept of the function of fiction. To add to the irony, the listeners watch a pretty young maid clearing the table of their teacups, and believe watching her is "better than any story" (IX, 37).

In commenting on this masterpiece, Thomas Gullason states that nothing is solved, but the story is like "a delayed fuse" that depends on "after-effects on the reader via the poetic technique of suggestion and implication."[44] In Chekhov's own comments on "Thieves," he maintained he would allow "the jury" to decide the "guilt" of the characters and would avoid "sermonizing" (Yarmolinsky, 133), but in "Gooseberries," the character of Ivan seems to occupy the role of the prosecuting attorney. The idea that Chekhov could use the character of Ivan in this manner, and yet avoid didacticism, is implied in Gullason's further comment that the story seems "as artless, as unplanned, as unmechanical as any story can be; it seems to be going nowhere, but it is going everywhere" (27). Chekhov achieves the effect of the master artist in creating the illusion that the story is artless, as episodic as life itself, while presenting a moral content as well-defined and as detailed as in any story he wrote.

That search for meaning in life is the subject of Chekhov's most complex and accomplished novella written in the first person: "My Life—A Provincial's Story" (Hingley). The narrating protagonist Misail Poloznev, one of Chekhov's most compelling characters, embodies that search for the authentic life with his honesty and his integrity. As the subtitle suggests, the story is a portrayal of provincial life, Chekhov's most extensive effort in prose in that direction, and the limiting nature of that life is explored in depth. One situation involves the tension that family relationships generate. The twenty-five-year old son of the town architect, Misail is considered a failure because he cannot retain a clerk's position, although it requires no "mental effort, talent, special ability or creative drive" (VIII, 118). Since he despises the work, he has been fired nine times. Chekhov's characters frequently turn to work in their search for an authentic life, but that work must be meaningful labor. After his last dismissal, Misail wishes to find such meaning through manual labor, but his typically middle-class father is ashamed that Misail would do such work, believing it is the "hallmark of slaves and barbarians" (VIII, 116). In the ensuing argument, the father beats Misail with an umbrella, causing a permanent break between them. The tension involves more than manual labor, for Misail believes his father is an incompetent architect because his imagination is "muddled, chaotic, stunted"— another example of the limiting nature of provincial life. Not only does Misail rebel, but when his sister Cleopatra discovers her provincial, middle-class life to be inauthentic, she does also.

Misail finds manual labor as a house painter, working for a Dickens-like character named Radish. Chekhov's portrayal of the laboring men and their attitudes toward life, each other, and the townspeople illustrates a broad knowledge of life. Misail's ideas on the meaning of life are articulated in a dialogue with another of Chekhov's doctor figures, Dr. Blagovo, whom Misail believes to be the "best and most cultivated" man in town. Like the dialogues in "In Exile" and "Ward Number Six," the philosophic positions of both characters are dramatized in lengthy conversations. Where Blagovo believes the "gray and commonplace" concerns of present life are not worth one's effort, Misail is committed to improving society. He is afraid "the art of enslavement" is gradually being perfected in the modern world, and believes although serfdom has been abolished, capitalism is spreading, so that "the majority still feeds, clothes and protects the minority, while remaining hungry, unclothed and unprotected itself" (VIII, 139). Misail also believes every man should do manual work, a belief similar to the artist's in "An Artist's Story," published earlier in the same year of 1896. Like in "An Artist's Story," Chekhov's artistic achievement in "My Life" lies not in articulating such ideas, but in creating emotionally complex characters capable of thinking deeply and passionately about the nature of man and society.

One aspect of the search for an authentic life in "My Life" involves love. Masha Dolzhikov, the daughter of a wealthy railway builder, falls in love with and marries Misail. Masha, who in contrast to the other provincials has lived in St. Petersburg, is an idealist who shares Misail's belief that rich and educated people should work like everyone else. She and Misail occupy one of her father's estates, where she attempts to live a meaningful life by farming. Misail knows Masha is not committed to a laboring life, for she has other choices with her wealth, but against his better judgment, he falls unequivocally in love with her. Chekhov's portrayal of the suffering this love causes Misail is one of the great accomplishments of the novella. The love between Misail and Masha is complemented by the love between Cleopatra and Dr. Blagovo, who has left his estranged wife and children in St. Petersburg. Cleopatra's love for the doctor incites her to seek an authentic life. In typical Chekhovian fashion, neither of these love relationships endure.

The relationship between Misail and Masha becomes dependent on her success with the estate. In contrast to Lydia in "An Artist's Story," Masha becomes disillusioned in attempting to build a school for the peasants. Chekhov's portrayal of her efforts and the peasants' response illustrate the immense difficulty of effecting change in society; one of Chekhov's many achievements in this novella is presenting that complex relationship between landowner and peasant. The peasant is presented sympathetically through the attitudes of Misail, for through plowing, harrowing, and sowing, he develops some sense of the "barbarous, brute force" that both confronts the peasant and is a part of him. Misail, drawn to the peasants, concludes they are a "highly strung, irritable people" who have had a raw deal and whose imaginations have been "crushed" (VIII, 170). For all the limitations of the peasants, Misail sees something vital and significant in them, something that is "lacking in Masha and the doctor for instance" (VIII, 170). That element is the belief in the truth, and the power of the truth to save not only the peasant himself, but all mankind. Misail believes the peasant "loves justice more than anything else in the world" (VIII, 170), a belief that connects Misail directly to Leo Tolstoy. As Ronald Hingley notes, no contemporary Russian reader would have missed the connection. (VIII, 5).

As the love relationship between Misail and Masha dissolves, she leaves for St. Petersburg, and then, before leaving for America, she requests a divorce. The other love relationship ends as Cleopatra dies shortly after giving birth to the doctor's child out of wedlock. In their last days, the suffering that Cleopatra and Misail endure in their poverty recalls the novels of Charles Dickens and Fyodor Dostoevsky. Like characters in those novels tried by circumstances, Misail experiences a mental breakdown from the emotional strain, and wanders the streets out of his mind.

After his recovery, in the final, expository chapter, Misail continues to work as a painter in town as he cares for his sister's child, like the narrator in "An Anonymous Story." In Misail's final comments, he declares the townspeople have been "reading and hearing about truth, mercy and freedom for generations" but "their entire progress from cradle to grave is one long lie"; they torment each other, "fearing and hating freedom as if it were their worst enemy" (VIII, 181). Chekhov thus links the relationship between the lie and freedom in this masterpiece. In commenting on "My Life," D. S. Mirsky states only one other story by Chekhov, entitled "In the Hollow," can rival it in terms of "poetical grasp" and significance (363).

The search for meaning in life in the provinces is also the subject of "On Official Business" (Hingley). The protagonist is a young coroner Lyzhin, who accompanies a doctor to a small village to investigate a suicide, the "official business" of the title. Once again, the limitations of provincial life are a theme. Because of a blizzard, Lyzhin must remain with the body for a number of hours in a hut, where he visits with the local constable, an old peasant who tells him about the dead man. After the peasant retires to another room, Lyzhin considers his life in this provincial outpost, contrasting it with the excitement of Moscow where he lived as a student, and decides "here you want nothing, you easily come to terms with your own insignificance, and you expect only one thing in life: just let it hurry up and go away" (IX, 117). If he could escape to Moscow in five or ten years, it still would not be too late to have a "whole life" ahead of him. To this point in the action, the events seem typical of many of Chekhov's stories about the limitations of provincial life, but events take a different direction when the doctor returns and invites Lyzhin to a local estate.

Lyzhin contrasts the gay happenings on the estate with the dismal peasant hut, feeling the difference between them is "magical." That night he dreams of the suicide and the old peasant marching together through the freezing cold and the deep snow, singing, "We know no peace, no joy. We bear all the burdens of this life, our own and yours" (IX, 122). When Lyzhin wakes, he realizes "some link—invisible, but significant and essential" (IX, 122) exists not only between the suicide and the old peasant, but between all men. Such a thought recalls "The Student," another story deceptively simple in its events, but in "On Official Business," the moral context of the idea is based in a secular humanism, without a Christian holiday as backdrop for the vision. Even in this remote backwater, Lyzhin realizes nothing is arbitrary, for "everything is imbued with a single common idea, everything has one spirit, one purpose" (IX, 122). This mystical thought occurs to an ordinary coroner, an undistinguished protagonist, and it suggests even ordinary man is capable of profound experiences. Lyzhin realizes reasoning is not enough to furnish these insights, but the gift of penetrating "life's essence" is required, and that gift is available to him who "sees and understands his own life as part of the common whole" (IX, 122). This vision of the individual's relationship to mankind serves as Chekhov's own moral position. The idea that the sense of man's responsibility to his fellow man could occur to such an ordinary man in such a remote backwater does not refute the limitations of provincial life, but illustrates the possibility that even here, man can exercise his human responsibility.

Chekhov's vision of mankind has a sociological dimension in "A Case History" (Hingley) written shortly before "On Official Business." The events are narrated through the consciousness of Dr. Korolyov, an assistant to a professor of medicine in Moscow, one of Chekhov's scientist doctors with a well-developed moral vision of the relationship between the individual and society. Society is represented by the setting of a factory town, similar to that in "A Woman's Kingdom," written four years previously; the stories share other similarities as well, one being the burden of social responsibility felt by the future heiress.

When Korolyov is summoned from Moscow to treat the owner's daughter, he ascertains her primary problem is not physiological but "nerves." Her symptoms are an indication of her inauthentic life, for like Anne in "A Woman's Kingdom," this young woman will inherit the vast mill with all its responsibility and she is "worried and scared" without understanding the reason. Her problem is she does not believe she has "the right" to be a mill owner and rich heiress, and Korolyov tells her that her insomnia is a good sign because it shows concern about right and wrong. Korolyov has a moral vision of the age: the previous generation was not bothered by such moral questions, and future generations will have solved them. In his belief in the future—"Life will be good in fifty years' time" (IX,77)—he resembles other optimistic doctors in Chekhov's work.

Korolyov's most profound thoughts on the nature of man and society develop as he strolls around the mill that evening. He had never visited a factory before, and previously had compared improvements in the workers' lives to the treatment of incurable diseases. The situation is so hopeless for the worker and/or the patient that he can only be made as comfortable as possible and never really healthy or cured. But now Korolyov realizes not only the workers, but the supervisors and the "bosses" are all involved in a labor in which the "principal, the main beneficiary, is the devil" (IX, 75).

Korolyov actually does not believe in the devil, but the image comes to mind because of the appearance of the mill fires at night. He imagines in the chaos of everyday life, some malevolent, mysterious force has forged the relationship between weak and strong so that both are "equal victims." Like the mutually harmful relationship between master and slave, the strong as well as the weak are victims of the "primitive mindless force" (IX, 75) that rules mankind.

With this vision, Korolyov functions as a metaphor for a spiritual doctor, "accustomed to forming accurate diagnoses of incurable chronic ailments deriving from some unknown ultimate cause" (IX, 74), with society as the sick patient, suffering from the malevolent, mysterious force that creates the illness in man's relationship to his fellow man. On one level, "On Official Business" complements this earlier story, for the coroner's vision of the common bond among men with its "one spirit, one purpose" becomes an answer, a cure, to the metaphoric illness that Korolyov diagnoses.

Stories of the Peasant

During this last period Chekhov wrote two masterpieces with peasant village life as his primary subject, "Peasants" and "In the Hollow." After appearing in 1897 in a literary journal, "Peasants" was printed as a separate volume with "My Life" and became very popular, with seven reprints in the following few years. Where the narrator in "My Life" is from the middle class and views the peasant in an objective, but sympathetic manner, in "Peasants" Chekhov mainly presents the peasants' experiences directly to the reader. The second masterpiece, "In the Hollow," resembles "Peasants" in that the characters and events also are presented directly through Chekhov's narrator. "The New Villa" (Hingley) is an important, chronologically intermediate story that gives the landowner and the peasant equal weight. The landowners in this story are a railway engineer and his compassionate wife who have recently moved to the area and built a new villa. They attempt to forge a relationship of integrity with the peasants in a neighboring village, but some of the peasants constantly take advantage of the engineer. In disgust, the engineer leaves the villa with his family and sells the estate.

The events provide insight into the difficulties of communication between both individuals and social groups. The goodwill efforts of two sets of characters—the engineer and his family, and a peasant blacksmith and his family—are defeated by the attitudes and actions of other hostile peasants. A new owner of the villa behaves much worse toward the peasants than the original compassionate owners, but the peasants get along with him much better. In one scene, the peasants pass the villa and wonder why they get along so well with the new owner, but knowing no answer, they "trudge on silently, heads bowed" (IX, 107). This image, when well-meaning people are defeated by some powerful force that operates against the betterment of human relations, is a powerful comment on the mysteriousness of human affairs.

If the portrait of peasant conditions that emerges from "The New Villa" is not encouraging, then the portrait in "Peasants" (Hingley) is a downright bleak naturalistic picture of unrelenting poverty that grinds down the human spirit. The portrayal is so unrelenting that Leo Tolstoy is reported to have termed it "a sin against the common people,"[45] but in Russia during Chekhov's own lifetime, "Peasants" was the most famous of all his stories. Ronald Hingley believes the story clearly is "a great work of art," and "a work of genius" (VIII, 3).

Brutal violence and indignities characterize life in a small peasant village of some forty huts. The narrative is a succession of hardship scenes with only an occasional experience to relieve the bleakness. A terminally ill waiter, Nicholas, returns from Moscow with his wife Olga and their ten-year-old daughter to live with his parents and his brother's families, all in one hut. When they arrive, Nicholas "actually took fright" as he sees how dark, cramped and dirty the hut is, recognizing the "real poverty and no mistake" (VIII, 196).

Later that first day, Nicholas and Olga have the opportunity to enjoy the beauty in the natural surroundings, but then Nicholas' drunk brother Kiryak comes to the hut and punches his wife Marya in the face. Pleased at the fear he causes, Kiryak drags Marya out of the hut "bellowing like a wild animal to make himself more frightening still" (VIII, 198). As usual in cases of domestic violence, Kiryak's beatings increase in intensity, and later are so severe that Marya has to be doused with water to bring her back to consciousness. Another instance of violence occurs as Kiryak himself is taken off to be flogged by the authorities.

The characters experience other disheartening indignities. Fyokla, another sister-in-law whose husband is away in the army, also lives in the hut with her children. One night she is stripped naked by the neighboring estate's servants, with many of whom she has been having sexual relations, and is left to wander home alone. When she returns, she weeps for her debasement. Another moving scene occurs when Nicholas' mother, Gran, who works hard to provide for the family, verbally abuses Nicholas. The samovar, their pot for heating tea water and symbol of the household, has been taken to pay taxes. Although she loves Nicholas, she feels so degraded and insulted when this happens she unfairly blames his family's presence for the misfortune. Since the members of the family have no one to turn to for help, they are completely vulnerable to these sufferings and hardships.

Although the events of the novella are narrated primarily through Chekhov's persona, certain passages are presented through the sensibility of Nicholas' wife Olga. As a newcomer, she notices behavior and detail that would not consciously register with the other characters. After a few months, Olga realizes life in the village is such a struggle that little time or effort is allowed for people to behave with anything but "mutual disrespect, fear and suspicion." But for all the hardship, Olga learns these people have a sense of community. When Kiryak is taken off to be flogged, Olga remembers "how pitiful and crushed the old people had looked" (VIII, 221).

During the middle of winter, Nicholas dies, and that spring Olga decides to return to Moscow, to secure a position as housemaid. As the novella closes, she and her daughter are walking to Moscow, begging for alms. Chekhov employs his objective technique in this scene so that the effect paradoxically provides the reader with a sense of intimacy with these destitute characters.

The sociological information contained in "Peasants" created a political uproar among parts of society, generating the kind of public response that recalled the appearance of a new novel by Ivan Turgenev or Fyodor Dostoevksy in previous times (Simmons, 393). The artistic value of the novella, however, derives from the validity of the characters and from the experience of village life that Chekhov depicts. Chekhov's portrayal of Fyokla's sensibility and motivation is superb, and there are a number of powerful, lyrical descriptions. One is a fire scene when one of the village huts burns; another is the peasants' response to the visit of a traveling religious procession and another is the simple experience of attempting to sleep in the crowded hut. Since there is no sharp dramatic conflict, the narrative becomes a succession of mosaics that remains etched in the reader's mind.

Since the characters of "In the Hollow" (Hingley) are engaged in a dramatic conflict, the form is more traditional. In contrast to the beautiful natural surroundings in "Peasants," the setting for this village is, as the title suggests, in the bottom of a ravine. Chekhov's environmental concerns are evident here where the village water is polluted by a tannery factory and the air always smells of factory waste, as if it were "clogged by a dense miasma of sin" (IX, 155). Unlike "Peasants," which focuses on a poor family, the subject for "In the Hollow" is the members of the family that operate the village store, the Tsybukins, the wealthiest family in the village. The head of the family is a clever old man who has built up his business by constantly cheating his peasant customers. In addition to illegal vodka, Tsybukin sells putrid salt beef before feast days, "stuff with so vile a stench you could hardly go near the barrel" (IX, 155). But Tsybukin does love his family, especially his eldest son Anisim, now a police detective in Moscow, and his daughter-in-law Aksinya, a "beautiful, well-built" peasant married to his younger son, a mentally impaired deaf man. The basic family situation in this novella recalls "Peasant Women," and in many ways "In the Hollow" develops from where the earlier story ends: the tensions in the family relationships, unresolved in "Peasant Women," are worked dramatically through in "In the Hollow" until the dissatisfied daughter-in-law controls the family.

Aksinya is one of Chekhov's most sinister characters, an ambitious woman with an unusual head for business. She operates the store as effectively and dishonestly as her father-in-law. Chekhov often uses the image of the snake in describing her; like a viper, she is physically dangerous, eventually killing her sister-in-law's baby in a fit of rage. In contrast to her dishonesty is the goodness of Barbara, Tsybukin's second wife; cheerful and lighthearted, she freely gives alms to beggars and various pilgrims who stop at the store. Another sister-in-law, Lipa, is a poor, self-effacing, but physically attractive peasant girl whom the eldest son Anisim marries on a return trip to the village. While the guests at this major event are feasting at table, a crowd of poor peasants gathers in the store yard. Occasionally when the band is not playing, one village woman's cry carries clearly to the table: "Rotten swine, grinding the faces of the poor. May you rot in hell!" (IX, 163). This cry of protest recalls Misail's comment in "My Life" on the desire of the peasant for justice. By the end of the novella, Lipa emerges as a symbol of the peasant. Both a victim and an endurer of wrongdoing, she joins that mosaic of suffering depicted in "Peasants."

The novella's key dramatic event occurs several months after Anisim is arrested for counterfeiting money. Ironically, Anisim's dishonest behavior was learned from his father. When Tsybukin returns from the sentencing of his son to Siberia, he wills some land to his grandson, the baby of Lipa and Anisim, but Aksinya is operating a brick factory on this land, and flies into a rage. In one of the most memorable scenes in Chekhov's work, she scalds the baby with boiling wash water. Once again, Chekhov uses irony: the action taken to help the baby instead destroys it. As Lipa attempts to come to terms with her grief, she wanders the countryside with the dead baby in her arms and questions the meaning of suffering in her simple, eloquent language.

In the final section, which occurs three years later, Lipa's character is once again juxtaposed against the members of the family. Aksinya has become the head of the house since Tsybukin is becoming feeble-minded, in part from grief. Aksinya is now a force in the community because of her brick factory; her power attracts the ardor of a local landowner. As Lipa passes through the village with a group of peasants who work in Aksinya's brickyard, she gives Tsybukin something to eat. This act, symbolic of her human compassion, is juxtaposed against the thriving dishonesty of the very family that threw her out, and is Chekhov's final use of irony in the novella. In commenting on the complexity and power of "In the Hollow," V. S. Pritchett pairs it with "The Bishop" as one of Chekhov's two "surpassing masterpieces" (178).

Stories of Religion

During this period Chekhov wrote two stories about characters committed to a religious life, stories in many ways diametrically opposed and indicative of Chekhov's great range as a writer. The characters in "Murder" (Hingley), Chekhov's most sensational story, are members of a fundamentalist religion who, in a frenzy of rage generated by frustration, beat a member of their household to death. The narrative begins in the consciousness of the victim, Matthew Terekhov, a laborer whose primary pleasures are attending church and singing in the choir. The element that makes his character so appropriate for the events that befall him is Matthew himself is a former religious fanatic, reared in a fundamentalist family like his cousin Jacob. After Matthew left home as a youth, he became increasingly devoted until he crossed over into fanaticism, doing penance such as going barefoot in the snow, wearing irons, and dragging around heavy stones. He established his own church where members went into "crazy fits" of shouting and dancing until they dropped. In one such service, Matthew committed fornication and when he requested forgiveness from his landlord, the man admonished Matthew to be an "ordinary man," for "overdoing things is devil's work" (VIII, 52). Matthew eventually responded to that guidance, and now does everything—"eat, drink *and* worship"—like everyone else.

Because of this experience, Matthew criticizes his cousin Jacob's religious practices. Jacob believes the churches are observing the rites incorrectly, and spends his time in special fasts and prayer sessions. In describing Jacob, Chekhov employs one key detail that resembles his later description of Belikov in "A Hard Case": both men wear galoshes all the time. Like Belikov, Jacob desperately clings to the "rules" because of his fear of life. Jacob's devotion is not to receive benefits from God, but for "form's sake"—upholding decorum, the same motivation of Belikov. During Easter week, when Jacob feels his faith leaving him and cannot worship as before, the stage is set for confrontation. Matthew implores Jacob to reform and accuses him of evil because he maintains a tavern at the inn where they live.

The murder is related with clever use of detail, revealing that Chekhov could be a superb writer of physical action, a fact often overlooked because so many of his stories are concerned with psychological action. One reason the scene is so effective is the unpremeditated manner in which the event unfolds. Like so much domestic violence, an argument simply gets out of hand. Jacob's sister engages Matthew in an argument about the use of oil on his food, forbidden during Lent, and Jacob joins the argument. Ironically, this day of religious observance becomes the scene for a deadly disagreement. Growing increasingly angry, Jacob grabs Matthew to drag him from the table, and in the confusion, the sister believes Matthew is attacking Jacob; she slams the bottle of oil down on Matthew's head, rendering him semiconscious. Jacob, who is "very worked up," props Matthew up and, pointing to the flat iron beside the table, directs his sister to hit him again. In their fury, they beat Matthew to death, not realizing what is happening until it is too late.

A year later, after the trial, Jacob is disgusted at his former religion—"it seemed irrational and primitive" (VIII, 67). But in a situation that recalls the events in "God Sees the Truth, But Waits" (1872) by Leo Tolstoy, Jacob, while in prison, eventually turns to God and the "true faith" once again. Like many of Chekhov's characters, Jacob now wants "to live." His heart aches with longing for his home, and he wants to return to tell people about his new faith.[46] Ivan Bunin, a short story writer especially sensitive to technique, thought this story the best of Chekhov's later work because the "objective narrator lets the shocking conduct make a great impact upon the reader" (Meister, 117).

Another masterpiece involving a character's commitment to religion is "The Bishop" (Hingley). Part of the power of the narrative derives from the subtle portrayal of an intelligent man's perceptions, his mind and emotions. In contrast to the characters in "Murder," the bishop is a reasonable and learned man with a good grasp of humankind who becomes annoyed during service by "the occasional shrieks of some religious maniac in the gallery" (IX, 191). Born into relative poverty, the bishop worked his way up to a position of power and influence and is now a distinguished figure, one of Chekhov's most elevated characters. The events are structured around his final struggle and test, typhoid fever. Appropriately enough, given the spiritual nature of the protagonist, the time is Easter week: the passions of the traditional religious ceremony are an effective backdrop for the protagonist's own emotional experiences. This story and "Easter Eve" are the crowning achievements of the Easter stories Chekhov had written since early in his career.

The focus is the bishop's evaluation of his life, a process initiated by the visit of his mother when she appears unexpectedly on the eve of Palm Sunday during his service. That evening his mind is filled with delight in recalling his poor native village and happy childhood, memories that his mother's appearance has triggered. The sheer delight with which the details are remembered—"the wheels creaking, sheep bleating, church bells pealing on bright summer mornings" (IX, 193)—recalls the thoughts of the character Gusev in his feverish state. The bishop is unknowingly developing typhoid fever, and like "Gusev" (1890), where the mind of the ill character is filled with memories before he eventually dies, the bishop's mind increasingly alters with his feverish state. The impressionistic prose is a development from those earlier depictions of altered states of consciousness in "Typhus" and "Sleepy."

During the next few days, as the bishop performs his administrative duties, he reflects on the "pettiness and pointlessness" of his tasks. The church ladies seem "tiresomely stupid," the peasants rough, the theological students ill-educated, and the paperwork overwhelming. The bishop is experiencing that particularly modern day Chekhovian test: instead of fire or sword, he must fight the trifles of everyday life, the "sheer weight" of which is dragging him down.

During the week, the bishop's illness progresses until he experiences the desire to escape and become a simple priest or ordinary monk, for his position seems to "crush" him. After he suffers an intestinal hemorrhage, he is diagnosed with typhoid fever, and in his weakness, he feels his past has escaped from him "to some infinitely remote place beyond all chance of repetition or continuation" (IX, 203). A sense of past provides a sense of identity, and so as the bishop desires, his identity is now dissolving. At this moment, his mother kisses him like a "dearly beloved child," and with her soothing presence, he feels like an "ordinary simple man walking quickly and cheerfully through a field," as "free as a bird" so he can go where he likes (IX, 203–204). Released at last from his worldly responsibilities, the bishop dies, symbolically just before dawn on Holy Saturday. The lyrical description of that joyful Easter Sunday captures the traditional rising of the spirit in Christian ritual as the continuity of the life process is thus assured. Chekhov relates in the closing paragraph no one remembered the bishop anymore except his mother, who lives in a remote province. His desire to become "ordinary" is fulfilled.

The subject of this masterpiece seems particularly appropriate for Chekhov at this stage in his life, when he himself was dying and confined to Yalta. That he should convert such personal materials into this work of art when writing itself was becoming an increasingly physically demanding task marks his great dedication as an artist.

Notes to Part 1

1. *Anton Chekhov's Life and Thought: Selected Letters and Commentary*, trans. Michael Heim in collaboration with Simon Karlinsky; selection, commentary and introduction by Simon Karlinsky (Berkeley: University of California Press, 1975), 367; hereafter cited in text.

2. Quoted in Ernest J. Simmons, *Chekhov: A Biography* (Boston: Little Brown, 1962), 73; hereafter cited in text.

3. Quoted in Vladimir Yermilov, *Anton Pavlovich Chekhov, 1860–1904*, trans. Ivy Litvinov (Moscow: Foreign Language Publishing House, n.d. [1956]), 55–6; hereafter cited in text.

4. *The Life and Letters of Anton Tchekhov*, trans. and ed. S. S. Koteliansky and Philip Tomlinson (London: Cassell & Co. Ltd., 1925; rpt: New York: Benjamin Blom, 1965), 146; hereafter cited in text.

5. Donald Rayfield, *Chekhov: The Evolution of His Art* (New York: Barnes and Noble, 1975), 26; hereafter cited Rayfield in text.

6. Karl Kramer notes that the Russian terminology to describe various forms of short fiction differs from the English. *The Chameleon and the Dream: The Image of Reality in Cexov's Stories* (The Hague: Mouton, 1970), 14–15. Hereafter cited in text. Simon Karlinsky comments: "The tenuous line that divides a long short story from a short novel makes the classification of Chekhov's fiction difficult in English (in Russian, the term *povest*, meaning a genre halfway between the story and the novel, does the job nicely)" (Heim, 201).

7. The close relationship between Chekhov's early prose comedy and his early drama is discussed by Vera Gottlieb in *Chekhov and the Vaudeville: A Study of Chekhov's One-Act Plays* (Cambridge: Cambridge University Press, 1982); hereafter cited in text.

8. Chekhov used the character of the drunkard in "In the Autumn" as a basis for his one-act play *On the High Road*. This play was banned by a censor because of its portrayal of the destitute aristocrat and was not performed during Chekhov's lifetime.

9. *Letters of Anton Chekhov to His Family and Friends with Biographical Sketch*, trans. Constance Garnett (New York: Macmillan, 1920), 301.

10. *Letters of Anton Chekhov* (New York: Viking Press, 1973), ed. Avrahm Yarmolinsky, 210; hereafter cited in text.

11. Chekhov's revision of stories for various editions after their appearance in the original magazine, and especially his revisions for his collected stories in 1899, make his artistic development difficult to chart accurately for the English reader. When Chekhov went through his early stories for the collected edition, he included only twenty stories from 1883—not one published before then. The Ecco edition of the Garnett translations carries the complete list of stories Chekhov included and most of the stories he omitted: "Chekhov's Stories: A Chronology," in *The Tales of Chekhov*, vol. 13 (New York: Ecco, 1987), 303–337;

hereafter cited in text. By 1899, Chekhov was an accomplished writer with almost twenty years of publishing experience who had developed a poetics over the course of his life that often led him to recast his early, original text. For an analysis of the kind of changes that Chekhov could make in a story, see the comment on "Fat and Thin" (Miles) by Abram Derman, "The Essence of Cexov's Creative Approach," in *Anton Chekhov as a Master of Story-Writing: Essays in Modern Soviet Literary Criticism*, trans. and ed. Leo Halunciski and David Savignac (The Hague: Mouton, 1976), 31–33.

12. Ronald Hingley, *A New Life of Anton Chekhov* (New York: Knopf, 1976), 82.

13. Back cover of *Tales of Chekhov*, vol. 13.

14. This version of "Difficult People" is the revision for Chekhov's collected stories, made fifteen years after the publication. As Donald Rayfield, explains in discussing the differences between the two versions, in this final version the story remains unresolved, neither father nor son in the right (57).

15. Chekhov and Tolstoy became friends after a meeting in August of 1895, almost nine years after "Excellent People" was published. Although each had reservations about the other's philosophy of life, they liked each other very much as individuals and admired each other greatly as writers. They continued to meet intermittently for as long as Chekhov lived.

16. D. S. Mirsky, *A History of Russian Literature*, ed. Francis J. Whitfield (New York: Knopf, 1926, 1969), 361; hereafter cited in text.

17. *Letters on the Short Story, the Drama, and Other Literary Topics*, sel. and ed. Louis S. Friedland, with a preface by Ernest Simmons (New York: Minto Beach, 1924; rpt. New York: Benjamin Blom, 1964), 69.

18. Quoted in Walter H. Buford, *Chekhov and His Russia: A Sociological Study* (2d. ed., London: Routledge and Kegan Paul, 1948; rpt. Hamden, Conn.: Archon Books, 1971), xiii–ix.

19. A. P. Chudakov, *Chekhov's Poetics*, trans. Edwina Cruise and Donald Dragt (Ann Arbor: Ardis, 1983), 6; hereafter cited in text. David Magarshack comments, "The dialogue in Chekhov's stories is essentially dramatic dialogue. . . . Many of these short stories, particularly the early ones, have been adapted for the Russian stage, but the 'adaptation' consisted mainly in lifting Chekhov's dialogue and using the descriptive passages as stage directions. Chekhov himself 'adapted' five of his short stories for the stage on the same principle, that is, he merely lifted the dialogue, adding his own stage directions, and, if his story was too short, expanding it to the necessary length" (*Chekhov the Dramatist* [New York: Hill and Wang, 1960], 20).

20. Charles B. Trimmer, "The Bizarre Element in Chekhov's Art," in *Anton Cechov 1860–1960: Some Essays*, ed. Thomas Eekman (Leiden: Brill, 1960), 281.

21. Renato Poggioli, "Storytelling in a Double Key," in *The Phoenix and the Spider* (Cambridge, Mass.: Harvard University Press, 1957), 123.

22. Gleb Struve, "On Chekhov's Craftsmanship: The Anatomy of a Story," *Slavic Review* 20 (1961): 466; hereafter cited in text.

23. This preference gains strength as the art involved in the short story form is more widely recognized. The novel has traditionally drawn more serious critical attention, and since the novella is more similar to the novel in form, historically most critics have preferred Chekhov's novellas. In attempting to explain the difference, Struve quotes Tolstoy that as an artist, Chekhov "can not even be compared with previous Russian writers—with Turgenev, Dostoevsky, or myself" (472). Chekhov, Tolstoy believed, had his "own peculiar manner, like the Impressionists" (472). His analogy to the movement in painting has validity as Nicholas Moravcevich aptly illustrates in tracing Chekhov's relationship with the painter Issak Ilich Levitan (1860–1900) ("Chekhov and Naturalism: From Affinity to Divergence," *Comparative Drama* IV [Winter 1970–1]: 219–240). Hereafter cited in text.

24. Beverly Hahn groups "Sorrow" with "The Huntsman," "Misery," and "Easter Eve" as examples of this new poetic form, in which the details of the setting can generate a "metaphoric epiphany" (*Chekhov: A Study of the Major Stories and Plays* [Cambridge: Cambridge University Press, 1977], 50–51; hereafter cited in text.

25. Among the stories of religious characters that I have already discussed under another rubric are "An Encounter," in which the itinerant peasant Yefrem functions as a symbol of Christian virtue, and "A Day in the Country," in which the old cobbler Trenery also functions as a similar, although less obvious, symbol of Christian virtue.

26. Frank O'Connor, *The Lonely Voice: A Study of the Short Story* (Cleveland and New York: Meridian Books, World Publishing Co., 1965; rpt: New York: Harper & Row, 1985), 85.

27. Although not specifically suggested in the story, the requirements for a good hymn are similar to those for a sonnet, or even a short story: "everything must be harmonious, brief, and complete." The comments on brevity, on language, and on the power of the art form to move the reader resemble Chekhov's comments on his own short fiction.

28. Gottlieb views Chekhov's contribution to the Russian vaudeville stage as similar to his contribution to the comic genre story: "he 'humanized' the 'stock' characters and made them realistic, complex individuals" (44).

29. This trim structure was to reappear in short fiction in the United States in the second half of the twentieth century in stories by such writers as John Updike (b. 1932), Richard Yates (b. 1926), Raymond Carver (1938–1988), Jonathan Penner (b. 1940), and Mary Robison (b. 1949). In his preface to *Prize Stories 1988: The O. Henry Awards* (New York: Doubleday, 1988), editor William Abrahams remarks:

As before, there is a remarkable variety among the works—each has its excellence. What seems more noticeable, however, is the ancestral presence of that great master of the short story, Anton Chekhov. It becomes increasingly clear that his has been the dominating spirit in the twentieth-century story, in its authenticity, in its humane concerns, and its openness to experience. Consciously or not, for he has been with us so long that he can be taken for granted, we are all in his debt.

Raymond Carver's "Errand," this year's First Prize story, is a beautiful and affecting acknowledgement of that debt. (x)

Chekhov's "dominating spirit" is manifest in its varied forms in short fiction, which developed from his "openness of spirit."

30. "Chekhov," in *Nineteenth Century Russian Literature: Studies of Ten Russian Writers*, ed. John Fennell (Berkeley: University of California Press, 1973), 323.

31. "The Party" was revised in 1893 for republication with some substantial cuts; and then it was slightly revised again in 1901 for the collected edition. The Ronald Hingley translation contains the deleted material of 1893 and 1901; a comparison of the revised edition to the original is insightful for understanding Chekhov's craftsmanship. See *The Oxford Chekhov*, ed. and trans. Ronald Hingley (London: Oxford University Press, 1968–75), vol. 4, 251–262; hereafter cited in text by volume and page number. In his revisions, Chekhov opts for brevity, allowing the action to speak for itself. In "The Party," that action is primarily the psychological process of the protagonist's thought.

32. Two of the three short stories published between these two novellas, "Thieves" and "Gusev," are arguably masterpieces; since neither story treats the inauthentic life within a domestic setting, both are discussed later in the chapter.

33. "The Short Story and the Novel [1958]," in *Man as an End: A Defense of Humanism*, trans. Bernard Wall (New York: Farrar, Straus & Giroux, 1966), 181–2.

34. "Chekhov's 'A Woman's Kingdom': A Drama of Character and Fate," *Critical Essays on Anton Chekhov*, ed. Thomas Eekman (Boston: G. K. Hall, 1989), 92.

35. *The Letters of Katherine Mansfield*, ed. J. Middleton Murray (New York: Knopf, 1936), 355.

36. "Chekhov and the Modern Short Story," in *A Chekhov Companion*, ed. Toby W. Clyman (Westport, Conn.: Greenwood Press, 1985), 159.

37. V. S. Pritchett, *Chekhov: A Spirit Set Free* (New York: Random House, 1988), 97; hereafter cited in text.

38. "Defining the Short Story: Impressionism and Form," *Modern Fiction Studies*, 28 (Spring 1982): 16.

39. "On the Nature of the Comic in Chekhov," in *Critical Essays on Anton Chekhov*, ed. Thomas Eekman (Boston: G. K. Hall, 1989), 67.

40. *The Unknown Chekhov: Stories and Other Writings Hitherto Untranslated*, trans. and intro. Avraham Yarmolinsky (New York: The Noonday Press, 1954), 15.

41. Quoted in the Ecco Press fall catalog for 1990, 13.

42. *Times Literary Supplement*, 9 November 1916, 537a, quoted in Charles W. Meister, *Chekhov Criticism: 1880 Through 1986* (Jefferson, North Carolina: McFarland, 1988), 143; hereafter cited in text.

43. "Chekhov's Cast of Characters," in *A Chekhov Companion*, ed. Toby W. Clyman (Westport, Conn.: Greenwood Press, 1985), 83.

44. "The Short Story," *Short Story Theories*, ed. Charles May (Athens, Ohio: Ohio University Press, 1976), 27. Hereafter references will be cited with "Gullason" and page number.

45. Quoted in Meister, 123. Gleb Struve notes this opinion is not, however, documented in Tolstoy's own writing. *Chekhov: Seven Short Novels*, trans. Barbara Makanowitzky; introduction and prefaces by Gleb Struve (New York: Norton, 1971), 365–6. Hingley uses the quote in his introduction (VIII, 5), with the source from N. I. Gitovich, *Letopis zhizni i tvorchestva A. P. Chekhov* [Chronicle of the Life and Literary Activity of A. P. Chekhov] (Moscow, 1955), 821. In 1962, Ernest Simmons termed this Gitovich book "the most indispensible reference work for all aspects of Chekhov's life and writings" (642), but unfortunately, the book remains untranslated.

46. The closing events of "Murder" contain Chekhov's most realized portrait of Sakhalin Island in fiction. Some of Chekhov's prose non-fiction narratives such as "Yegor's Story," in *The Island: A Journey to Sakhalin*, trans. Luba and Michael Terpak; introduction by Robert Payne (New York: Washington Square Press, 1967), suggest the origins for characters such as Anisim from "In the Hollow," Yergunov in "Thieves" and Jacob Terekhov in "Murder." In his introduction to this translation, Robert Payne terms *The Island* "a strange work, brilliant and wayward, scrupulously honest and unpretentious, lit by a flame of quiet indignation and furious sorrow" (xxxvi).

Part 2

THE WRITER

Introduction

Since many of Chekhov's correspondents were editors and other writers, an occasional subject in his letters was the nature of his writing process. Although many of his comments are of a practical nature, about the work at hand or the work of other writers, he occasionally made statements about his larger concerns, goals, and intentions as a writer. Many of these remarks have been widely anthologized, and one complete volume, *Letters on the Short Story, the Drama, and other Literary Topics by Anton Chekhov*, selected and edited by Louis Friedland (New York: Benjamin Blom, Inc., 1964), is devoted to this subject.

The Russian literary critic D. S. Mirsky classifies Chekhov as one of the three best letter writers in Russian, and in his article "Chekhov as Correspondent" (in *The Chekhov Companion*), Thomas Eekman notes that the letters are "a true companion to Chekhov's works, a mirror to his life and times, his thinking, and his relationships with other people. Though unintentionally so, they are fascinating literature in their own right" (269). The enclosed selections have been edited to illustrate his specific thought on short fiction, and do not fully illustrate Chekhov's charm, his "slightly bantering, facetious, light, and lively spirit" (Eekman, 256). The standard translations of the letters are listed in a separate section in the bibliography.

In addition to the letters, Chekhov kept a working notebook for a few years of his life, published as *Notebook of Anton Chekhov* (New York: Ecco Press, 1987). Also, many of Chekhov's comments on writing have been recorded by friends from direct conversation; among the most interesting is Ivan Bunin, "Chekhov," in *Memories and Portraits* (Greenwood Press, 1968), 31–58. Chekhov wrote some of his most specific comments to Maxim Gorky, selections of which are included in this section; Gorky's impression of Chekhov and Chekhov's thought is available in "Chekhov," in *On Literature* (Seattle: University of Washington Press, 1973), 271–291.

In addition to Chekhov's direct statements on the art of fiction, his play *The Seagull* includes the insightful commentary by the writer character Trigorin.

Selected Letters

In March of 1886, Dmitry Grigorovich, a noted Russian novelist of the age, wrote Chekhov that he had a real gift for writing that he should respect, and urged him not to write so quickly but to save his best efforts for serious work. This excerpt is from Chekhov's response.

28 March 1886, to Dmitry Grigorovich:

If I have a gift that should be respected, I confess before the purity of your heart that hitherto I have not respected it. I felt that I did have talent, but I was used to thinking it insignificant. Purely external causes are enough to make one unjust to oneself, suspicious, and diffident. And, as I think of it now, there have been plenty of such causes in my case. All those who are near to me have always treated my writing with condescension and have never stopped advising me in a friendly manner not to give up real work for scribbling. I have hundreds of acquaintances in Moscow, among them a score or so of people who write, and I cannot recall a single one who would read me or regard me as an artist. In Moscow there is a Literary Circle, so-called: gifted writers and mediocrities of all ages and complexions meet once a week in a restaurant and give their tongues free rein. If I were to go there and read them even a fragment of your letter, they would laugh to my face. In the five years that I have been knocking about newspaper offices I have come to accept this general view of my literary insignificance; before long I got used to taking an indulgent view of my labors, and so the fat was in the fire. That's the first cause. The second is that I am a physician and am up to my ears in medical work, so that the saw about chasing two hares has robbed no one of more sleep than me. [The allusion is to the Russian proverb: chase two hares, and you catch neither.]

I am writing all this for the sole purpose of exonerating myself to at least some degree in your eyes. Up till now my attitude toward my literary work has been extremely frivolous, casual, thoughtless. I cannot think of a *single* story at which I worked for more than a day, and "The Huntsmen," which you liked, I wrote in a bathing-cabin. I wrote my stories the way reporters write notices of fires: mechanically, half-consciously, without caring a pin either about the reader or myself. . . . I wrote and tried my best not to use up on a story the images and scenes which are dear to me and which, God knows why, I treasured and carefully concealed.

What first impelled me to self-criticism was a very friendly and, I believe, sincere letter from Suvorin. I began to plan writing something decent, but I still lacked faith in my ability to produce anything worth while.

And then against all expectations came your letter. Excuse the comparison, but it had the effect on me of a governor's order to leave town within twenty-four hours: I suddenly felt the urgent need to hurry and get out of the hole in which I was stuck. . . .

I agree with you entirely. The instances of cynicism that you point out I myself recognized when I saw "The Witch" in print. Had I written the story in three or four days instead of in twenty-four hours, they would not have been there.

I will stop—but not soon—doing work that has to be delivered on schedule. It is impossible to get out of the rut I am in all at once. I don't object to going hungry, as I went hungry in the past, but it is not a question of myself. . . . To writing I give my leisure: two or three hours during the day and a fraction of the night, that is, an amount of time that is good only for short pieces. In the summer when I have more spare time and fewer expenses I shall undertake some serious piece of work.

Alexander Chekhov, Anton's older brother, was a working journalist who sent plans for a work to be titled "The City of the Future" to Anton for his opinion.

Part 2

10 May 1886, to Alexander Chekhov:

"The City of the Future" is a magnificent subject on account of both its novelty and its appeal. I think that if you overcome your laziness you will do rather well, but you are such a sloth! "The City of the Future" will be a work of art only on these conditions: (1) no politico-economico-social verbal effusions; (2) objectivity throughout; (3) truth in the description of characters and things; (4) extreme brevity; (5) audacity and originality—eschew clichés; (6) warmheartedness.

In my opinion, descriptions of nature should be extremely brief and offered by the way, as it were. Give up commonplaces, such as: "the setting sun, bathing in the waves of the darkening sea, flooded with purple gold," and so on, or: "Swallows, flying over the surface of the water, chirped gaily." In descriptions of nature one should seize upon minutiae, grouping them so that when, having read the passage, you close your eyes, a picture is formed. For example, you will evoke a moonlit night by writing that on the mill dam the glass fragments of a broken bottle flashed like a bright little star, and that the black shadow of a dog or a wolf rolled along like a ball, and so on. Nature becomes animated if you do not shrink from making physical phenomena resemble human actions.

In the area of mental states there are also particulars. May God save you from generalities. It is best to avoid descriptions of the mental states of your heroes; the effort should be to make these clear from their actions. Don't have too many characters. The center of gravity should be two: he and she.

4 October 1988, to A. N. Pleshcheyev (a noted poet and friend):

I am afraid of those who look for a tendency between the lines and who insist on seeing me as necessarily either a liberal or a conservative. I am not a liberal, not a conservative, not a gradualist, not a monk, not an indifferentist. I should like to be a free artist and nothing more, and I regret that God has not given me the power to be one. I hate lying and violence, whatever form they take. . . . Pharisaism, stupidity, and tyranny reign not in shopkeepers' homes and in lock-ups alone: I see them in science, in literature, in the younger generation. That is why I have no partiality either for gendarmes, or butchers, or scholars, or writers, or young people. I regard trade-marks and labels as prejudicial. My holy of holies is the human body, health, intelligence, talent, inspiration, love, and absolute freedom—freedom from force and falsehood, no matter how the last two manifest themselves. This is the program I would follow if I were a great artist.

4 May 1889, to A. S. Suvorin (a friend and powerful editor of the age who published many of Chekhov's masterpieces):

You write that I have grown lazy. This does not mean that I have become lazier than I was. I work now just as much as I worked three to five years back. To work, and to have the appearance of a man who works from nine in the morning until dinner and from evening tea until bedtime has become a habit with me, and in this respect I am a bureaucrat. But if my labor does not result in two novellas a month, or an income of ten thousand a year, it isn't laziness that is to blame but my psycho-physical make-up: I don't love money enough to go in for medicine in a big way, and as for literature, I am short on passion and, consequently, on talent. The flame within me burns evenly and sluggishly, without flare-ups and crackling; that's why I never happen to dash off three or four sheets at one sitting in a single night, or to get so carried away by my work as to hinder myself from going to bed if I want to sleep. Hence I commit neither outstanding stupidities nor do I perform outstanding feats of intelligence.

14 January 1887, to Maria Kiselyova (a family friend and writer of childrens' stories):

To a chemist there is nothing impure on earth. The writer should be just as objective as the chemist; he should liberate himself from everyday subjectivity and acknowledge that manure piles play a highly respectable role in the landscape and that evil passions are every bit as much a part of life as good ones.

30 May 1888, to A. S. Suvorin:

In my opinion it is not the writer's job to solve such problems as God, pessimism, etc.; his job is merely to record who, under what conditions, said or thought what about God or pessimism. The artist is not meant to be a judge of his characters and what they say; his only job is to be an impartial witness. I heard two Russians in a muddled conversation about pessimism, a conversation that solved nothing; all I am bound to do is reproduce that conversation exactly as I heard it. Drawing conclusions is up to the jury, that is, the readers. My only job is to be talented, that is, to know how to distinguish important testimony from unimportant, to place my characters in the proper light and speak their language . . .

11 September 1888, to A. S. Suvorin:

You advise me not to chase after two hares at once and to forget about practicing medicine. I don't see what's so impossible about chasing two hares at once even in the literal sense. Provided you have the hounds, the chase is feasible. In all likelihood I am lacking in hounds (in the figurative sense now), but I feel more alert and more satisfied with myself when I think of myself as having two occupations instead of one. Medicine is my lawful wedded wife, and literature my mistress. When one gets on my nerves, I spend the night with the other. This may be somewhat disorganized, but then again it's not as boring, and anyway, neither one loses anything by my duplicity. If I didn't have medicine, I'd never devote my spare time and thoughts to literature. I lack discipline.

27 October 1888, to A. S. Suvorin:

In conversations with my fellow writers I always insist that it is not the artist's job to try to answer narrowly specialized questions. It is bad for the artist to take on something he doesn't understand. We have specialists for dealing with special questions; it is their job to make judgments about the peasant communes, the fate of capitalism, the evils of intemperance and about boots and female complaints. The artist must pass judgment only on what he understands; his range is as limited as that of any other specialist—that's what I keep repeating and insisting upon. Anyone who says the artist's field is all answers and no questions has never done any writing or had any dealings with imagery. The artist observes, selects, guesses and synthesizes. The very fact of these actions pre-supposes a question; if he hadn't asked himself a question at the start, he would have nothing to guess and nothing to select. To put it briefly, I will conclude with some psychiatry: if you deny that creativity involves questions and intent, you have to admit that the artist creates without premeditation or purpose, in a state of unthinking emotionality. And so if any author were to boast to me that he'd written a story from pure inspiration without first having thought over his intentions, I'd call him a madman.

You are right to demand that an author take conscious stock of what he is doing, but you are confusing two concepts: *answering the questions* and *formulating them correctly*. Only the latter is required of an author. There's not a single question answered in *Anna Karenina* or *Eugene Onegin*, but they are still fully satisfying works because the questions they raise are all formulated correctly. It is the duty of the court to formulate the questions correctly, but it is up to each member of the jury to answer them according to his own preference. . . .

You write that the hero of my "Name-Day Party" is a figure worth developing. Good Lord, I'm not an insentient brute, I realize that. I realize I hack up my characters, ruin them, and I waste good material. To tell you the truth, I would have been only too glad to spend half a year on "The Name-Day Party." I like taking my own good time about things, and see nothing attractive about slapdash publication. I would gladly describe *all* of my hero, describe him with feeling, understanding and deliberation. I'd describe his emotions while his wife was in labor, the trial, his sense of disgust after being acquitted, I'd describe the midwife and doctors having tea in the middle of the night, I'd describe the rain. . . . It would be sheer pleasure for me, because I love digging deep and rummaging. But what can I do? I began the story on September 10th with the thought that I have to finish it by October 5th at the latest; if I miss the deadline I'll be going back on my word and will be left without any money. I write the beginning calmly and don't hold myself back, but by the middle I start feeling uneasy and apprehensive that the story will come out too long. I have to keep in mind that the *Northern Herald* is low in funds and that I am one of its more expensive contributors. That's why my beginning always seems as promising as if I'd started a novel, the middle is crumpled together and timid, and the end is all fireworks, like the end of a brief sketch. Whether you like it or not, the first thing you have to worry about when you're working up a story is its framework. From your mass of heroes and semi-heroes you choose one individual, a wife or a husband, place him against the background, and portray only that person and emphasize only him. The others you scatter in the background like so much small change. The result is something like the firmament: one large moon surrounded by a mass of tiny stars. But the moon doesn't work, because it can only be understood once the other stars are understandable, and the stars are not sufficiently delineated. So instead of literature I get a patchwork quilt. What can I do? I don't know. I have no idea. I'll just have to trust to all-healing time.

7 January 1889, to A. S. Suvorin:

There are other things no less necessary than talent and an abundance of material. Maturity, to begin with. Then, *a sense of personal freedom* is also quite indispensable. And this sense didn't begin growing inside me until very recently. I had never had it before, replacing it quite successfully with frivolity, carelessness and a lack of respect for my work.

What aristocratic writers take from nature gratis, the less privileged must pay for with their youth. Try and write a story about a young man—the son of a serf, a former grocer, choirboy, schoolboy and university student, raised on respect for rank, kissing the priests' hands, worshiping the ideas of others, and giving thanks for every piece of bread, receiving frequent whippings, making the rounds as a tutor without galoshes, brawling, torturing animals, enjoying dinners at the houses of rich relatives, needlessly hypocritical before God and man merely to acknowledge his own insignificance—write about how this young man squeezes the slave out of himself drop by drop and how, on waking up one fine morning, he finds that the blood coursing through his veins is no longer the blood of a slave, but that of a real human being.

25 November 1892, to A. S. Suvorin:

Bear in mind that writers who are considered immortal or just plain good and who intoxicate us have one very important trait in common: they are going somewhere and call you with them; you sense, not with your mind but with all your being, that they have an aim, like the ghost of Hamlet's father, who had a reason for appearing and alarming the imagination. Looking at some of them in terms of their calibre you will see that they have immediate aims—the abolition of serfdom, the liberation of their country, political matters, beauty, or just vodka, . . . ; others have remote aims—God, life beyond the grave, the happiness of mankind and so on. The best of them are realistic and paint life as it is, but because every line is saturated with juice, with the sense of life, you feel, in addition to life as it is, life as it should be, and you are entranced.

3 December 1898, to Maxim Gorky (Russia's foremost postrevolutionary writer):

You ask for my opinion of your stories. My opinion? You have undoubted talent, truly a genuine, immense talent. In your story "On the Steppe," for example, your talent is shown as extraordinarily powerful, and I even experienced a moment of envy that it was not I who had written it. You are an artist and a brilliant man. You feel things magnificently; you are plastic, i.e., when you depict a thing, you see it and touch it with your hands. That is true art. . . .

Now shall I speak of your defects? This is not so easy, though. Referring to shortcomings in the way of talent is like talking of the defects of a fine tree in an orchard; in the main it is certainly not a question of the tree itself but of the tastes of those who look at it. Isn't that so?

I will begin by pointing out that in my opinion you have no restraint. You are like a spectator in a theatre who expresses his rapture so unrestrainedly that he prevents himself and others from hearing. This lack of restraint is especially evident in your descriptions of nature, which break up the continuity of your dialogues; one would like these descriptions to be more compact and concise, just two or three lines or so. The frequent references to voluptuousness, whispering, velvet softness and so on lend a certain rhetorical quality and monotony to these descriptions, and they dampen one's enthusiasm and almost fatigue the reader. This lack of restraint is also evident in your characterizations of women ("Malva," "On the Rafts") and in love scenes. The effect you create is not of expansiveness nor of a broad sweep of your brush, but merely lack of restraint. Then, you make frequent use of words entirely unsuited to your kind of story. Accompaniment, disk, harmony—these words stand in the way of the narrative. You speak often of waves. There is a strained, circumspect effect in your portrayals of people of culture; it is not because you haven't observed them closely enough, for you do know them; it is that you don't exactly know how to tackle them.

3 January 1899, to Maxim Gorky:

Apparently you misunderstood me somewhat. I didn't refer to crudity of style, but merely to the incongruity of foreign, not truly Russian or rarely used words. In other authors words like "fatalistically," for instance, pass unnoticed, but your things are musical and well proportioned, so that every rough spot stands out like a sore thumb. Of course we are here concerned with a matter of taste and perhaps I am only expressing the excessive fastidiousness or conservatism of a man who has long been rooted in definite habits. . . .

Are you self-taught? In your stories you are the true artist, a real man of culture. Least of all is coarseness a quality of yours, you are understanding and you feel things subtly and sensitively. Your best works are "On the Steppe" and "On the Rafts"—did I write you so? These are superb pieces, models of their kind, obviously by an artist who has gone through a very good school. I do not think I am mistaken. The only defect is the lack of restraint, of grace. When a person expends the least possible quantity of movement on a certain act, that is grace. There is a feeling of excess, though, in your outlay of words.

The descriptions of nature are artistic; you are a genuine landscapist. Except that the frequent use of the device of personification (anthromorphism) when you have the sea breathe, the heavens gaze down, the steppe caress, nature whisper, speak or mourn, etc.—such expressions render your descriptions somewhat monotonous, occasionally oversweet and sometimes indistinct; picturesque and expressive descriptions of nature are attained only through simplicity, by the use of such plain phrases as "the sun came out," "it grew dark," "it rained,"etc. This simplicity is inherent in you to a degree rarely found among any of our writers.

3 September, 1899, to Maxim Gorky:

Here is more advice: when you read proof, take out adjectives and adverbs wherever you can. You use so many of them that the reader finds it hard to concentrate and he gets tired. You understand what I mean when I say, "The man sat on the grass." You understand because the sentence is clear and there is nothing to distract your attention. Conversely, the brain has trouble understanding me if I say, "A tall, narrow-chested man of medium height with a red beard sat on green grass trampled by passersby, sat mutely, looking about timidly and fearfully." This doesn't get its meaning through to the brain immediately, which is what good writing must do, and fast.

11 October 1899, to Grigori Rossolimo (a fellow student of Chekhov's in medical school who shared his interests in social problems):

My name is A. P. Chekhov and I was born on the 17th of January 1860 in Taganrog. My education began at the Greek school connected with the Emperor Constantine Church, after which I attended the Taganrog Boys' school. In 1879 I entered the medical school of Moscow University. At that time I only had a vague idea of the various courses and cannot recall what considerations led me to choose the medical course, but I do not now regret the choice. During my first year at the university I was already having things printed in the weekly newspapers and magazines, and by the early eighties these literary pursuits had assumed a regular, professional character. In 1888 I was awarded the Pushkin Prize. In 1890 I visited Sakhalin Island to write a book on our penal colony and prison system there. Excluding court reports, reviews, articles, notes, all the items composed from day to day in the newspapers and which would now be difficult to unearth and collect, in twenty years of literary activity I have set down on paper and had published more than forty-eight hundred pages of tales and stories. I have also written plays for the theatre.

My work in the medical sciences undoubtedly had a great influence on my writing; certainly it widened the area of my observations and enriched my knowledge, and only one who is himself a doctor can tell you how valuable that training has been. My medical background has also been a guide to me; I have probably managed to avoid many mistakes because of it. Familiarity with natural sciences and the scientific method has always kept me on my guard, and wherever possible I have tried to write on the basis of scientific data; where it was impossible, I preferred not to write. I may note incidentally that artistic considerations do not always allow me to write in complete harmony with scientific data; on the stage you cannot show death by poisoning as it actually occurs. But even in such a case one must be consistent with scientific data, i.e., the reader or spectator must clearly realize that certain conventions are responsible for what has been shown and that he is dealing with an author who knows what he is talking about. I am not in the same camp with literary men who take a skeptical attitude toward science; and I would not want to belong to those who handle every subject solely on the basis of their wits.

Part 3

THE CRITICS

Introduction

Chekhov has been blessed with the attention of a very large number of perceptive critics. In the first selection presented here, the well-known translator Avrahm Yarmolinsky provides an overview of Chekhov as a writer of short fiction with comment on specific characteristics appearing in individual stories. In addition to editing *The Portable Chekhov*, from which this selection was taken, he has edited *The Unknown Chekhov* (New York: The Noonday Press, 1954), which contains some Chekhov narratives unavailable elsewhere in English, and a large selection of the letters, listed in the bibliography.

In the second selection, taken from the introduction to the excellent *Letters of Anton Chekhov*, listed in the bibliography under the reprint title *Anton Chekhov's Life and Thought*, Simon Karlinsky analyzes two of Chekhov's primary subjects, religion and sex. This book provides some of the most detailed and accurate commentary on the letters available, and the introductions offer valuable insight into Chekhov as a writer of short fiction.

Avrahm Yarmolinsky

Chekhov's stories are by far the larger and the more rewarding, as well as the more influential portion of his work. He limited himself to the short narrative not without a struggle. When his writing first assumed a serious cast, he was harassed by the feeling that he was doing less than his best. Characters, situations, scenes were crowding his mind, begging to be realized: what weddings, what funerals, what splendid women! The unborn figments were jealous, as he put it, of those that had seen the light. But he was hoarding this wealth, he was not going to throw it away on trifles, he was going to save it for some substantial work, for a novel. And he did start the novel. He kept mentioning it in his letters. He called it: "Stories from the Lives of My Friends." In spite of the suspicious title, he insisted that it was not going to be a patchwork, but a composed whole. He even chose a dedicatee. And then, about 1891, all references to the work cease, and no trace of the manuscript has been found to this day. Now and again, in later years his desire to write a novel would reawaken, and indeed he did produce several long narratives, but not one of them quite achieves the stature of a novel.

Perhaps to account for his failure, Chekhov threw out the rather dubious suggestion that the writing of novels required a degree of cultivation, a mastery, a consciousness of personal freedom possessed only by members of the privileged classes, and that the art was beyond the powers of plebeians like himself. Aggravating the sense of his inadequacy was the belief that he belonged to a generation of epigoni, unworthy descendants of giants like Turgenev, Dostoevsky, Tolstoy. In any case, the short story remained his vehicle to the end. It offered a form admirably suited to his genius.

With few exceptions, the locale of his tales is the native one, their time that in which Chekhov himself lived, their approach realistic. Within these limits, their variety is enormous, taking in, as they do, men and

From: "Introduction," from *The Portable Chekhov* by Avrahm Yarmolinsky, editor. Copyright 1947, 1968 by Viking Penguin, Inc. Renewed copyright (c) 1975 by Avrahm Yarmolinsky. Used by permission of Viking Penguin, a division of Penguin Books USA Inc.

women, old and young, rich and poor, people in every station: peasants, landowners, priests, policemen, school teachers, prostitutes, doctors, merchants, government officials. The human comedy, at least a large part of it, is enacted in a series of short scenes, some of them farcical, many of them deeply tinged with pathos, a few verging on tragedy or having a touch of irony. The interest may attach to a simple situation, as in "Vanka," or it may lie in a complex of relations, as in "The Name-Day Party," or again it may center on a psychological type, as in "The Man in a Shell."

In his notebook Chekhov entered this quotation from Daudet: " 'Why are your songs so short?' a bird was asked. 'Is it because you are short of breath?' 'I have a great many songs and I should like to sing them all.' " He wrote seven or eight hundred stories. A large number of them, including much, though by no means all, of his best work and every one of his longer narratives, are available in English. He was an uneven writer. . . . Where he attempts a story involving action and suspense, one with a plot, a sharp point, a neat solution, the result is apt to be wanting in distinction. Probably his lack of dramatic instinct was responsible for this. Where, however, he uses the method that he made peculiarly his own, though it had been employed before his time by Turgenev and other Russians, he is one of the masters, and he shows his gifts often enough to embarrass an editor with riches.

The most characteristic of Chekhov's stories lack purely narrative interest. They no more bear retelling than does a poem. Nothing thrilling happens in them, nor are the few reflective passages particularly compelling. Some of the tales, having neither beginning nor end, are, as Galsworthy put it, "all middle like a tortoise." Others have a static quality, with no more progression than there is in a dance. Instead of moving toward a definite conclusion, they are apt to trail off or drop to an anti-climax. And yet they manage to take hold of the imagination in an amazing fashion. Precisely because of the lack of invention and contrivance, the absence of cleverness, the fact that the loose ends are not tucked up nor the rough edges beveled, and that they remain unfinished in more senses than one, they have the impact of a direct experience.

It lay within Chekhov's gift to create characters who have come to be a by-word in Russia. And this although the creatures of his imagination are somewhat shadowy, since he is inclined to sketch a type rather than to paint the portrait of an individual. He had an intimate understanding of the complexities, the non-sequiturs of the mind and particularly of the heart. His was an observant eye for the telling detail of appearance or behavior, for whatever would contribute to placing his characters within the proper physical or social setting. His stories have an atmosphere as distinct as an odor.

Chekhov's preoccupation is with existences that are commonplace, drab, narrow. The life he pictures is one in which there is cruelty, want, boredom, misunderstanding, with only an occasional interval of happiness or serenity, a rare intimation that justice and goodness may ultimately prevail—in sum, an unintelligible and largely painful business. A man and woman are involved with one another and can live neither together nor apart. A cabman loses his son and can find no one to give ear to his grief but his horse. A woman wastes her youth in the provinces. Human beings are broken by the machinery of the State. Chekhov's characters may long for something that would lend meaning and beauty to their existence, yet they do not act to bring that consummation nearer. Their frustration is apt to be the result of their own helplessness. Often we encounter them in the midst of their feeble struggles, or, already defeated, facing an impasse. Chekhov preached the gospel of work as the panacea for his country's ills, and his heart went out to non-conformists and to enterprising, courageous men, such as the explorers of the Russian North, and yet he was incapable of projecting successfully a fighter, a rebel, a man of steadfast purpose. It is as though he were so suspicious of power, associating it with its abuse, that he looked upon weakness with a forgiving, almost an affectionate eye. The situations he usually presents are at the opposite pole from melodrama, as is his style from the melodramatic. His language is simple, rather slovenly, with rare strokes of bold imagery, sometimes very expressive, always free from the emphatic, the rhetorical, the florid.

A man of a sober and naturalistic temper, Chekhov was dogged by the thought that our condition in this uncomfortable world is a baffling one. He liked to say that there was no understanding it. And, indeed, his writings heighten that sense of the mystery of life which is one of the effects of all authentic literature. At the same time they tend to discourage the view that existence is a meaningless play of chance forces. In "A Tedious Story," a work of his early maturity and one of the most somber pieces to have come from his pen, an old professor discovers to his deep distress that there is nothing in his thoughts and feelings that could be called "a general idea, or the god of living man." Chekhov's writings pay covert homage to such a life-giving idea. In the semblance of the image of beauty, of the impulse toward justice, of the ideal of saintliness, it glimmers through the daily commonplace. His men and women sometimes reach out for something "holy, lofty and majestic as the heavens overhead." On a few occasions he allows his characters intuitions tinged with mysticism. Thus "The Black Monk" is concerned, however ambiguously, with madness as the gateway to transcendental reality, and the examining magistrate in "On Official Business" is haunted by the thought that nothing is accidental or fragmentary in our existence, that "everything has one soul, one aim," that individual lives are all parts of an organic whole.

Like the student in "A Nervous Breakdown," Chekhov had a "talent for humanity"—a generous compassion that went hand in hand with understanding and with a profound regard for the health of body and soul. Asked to give his opinion about a story dealing with a syphilitic, he wrote to the author that syphilis was not a vice but a disease, and that those who suffer from it needed not censure but friendly care. It was a bad thing, he went on to say, for the wife in the story to desert her husband on the ground that he had a contagious or loathsome illness. "However," he concluded, "she may take what attitude she likes toward the malady. But the author must be humane to the tips of his fingers." Chekhov lived up to this precept.

Next to his humanity, his supreme virtue is his candor. He is no teller of fairy tales, no dispenser of illusory solaces or promises. He does not tailor his material to fit our sense of poetic justice or to satisfy our desire for a happy ending. In his mature years he clung to the conviction that a writer was not an entertainer, not a confectioner, not a beautician, but a man working under contract who was bound by his conscience to tell the whole truth with the objectivity and the indifference to bad smells of a chemist. At the same time he was plagued, as has been seen, by a feeling of his insufficiency. He lived, he protested, in "a flabby, sour, dull time," and he had, like the rest of his generation, no goals toward which to lead his readers, no enthusiasm with which to infect them. And so he assigned to himself the modest role of a reporter, a witness, a man who, without presuming to solve any problems, merely posed them or recorded, to the best of ability, the way others posed them.

He was indeed an incorruptible witness, but he did not remain in the witness box all the time. Implicit in his writings is a judgment against cruelty, greed, hypocrisy, stupidity, snobbery, sloth—all the slavish traits he had been at pains to squeeze out of himself, against whatever degrades man and prevents him from achieving his full stature. Notwithstanding his protestations of objectivity, and though his attitude toward evil was not so much active hatred as abhorrence, there is indignation and indictment in his pages, a thinly veiled criticism of life. He even succumbs to the Russian weakness for preachment. There is no doubt that eventually he came to expect a corrective influence from his plays and stories. By telling the truth, he said to himself, he would help men to live more decently. "Man will become better when you show him what he is like," runs an entry in his notebook. One need not have faith in human perfectibility to acknowledge that there is something liberating and exalting in a frank facing of man's estate.

Simon Karlinsky

"Between the statements of 'God exists' and 'There is no God' lies a whole vast field, which a true sage crosses with difficulty. But a Russian usually knows only one of these two extremes; what lies between them is of no interest to him and he usually knows nothing or very little." This maxim is to be found in Anton Chekhov's private notebooks not once, but several times. The tyrannical and pharisaic religious upbringing which Chekhov's father forced on his children resulted in a loss of faith by every single one of them once they became adults. While Anton did not turn into the kind of militant atheist that his older brother Alexander eventually became, there is no doubt that he was a nonbeliever in the last decades of his life. But his early religious upbringing never quite left him and it is very much in evidence both in his correspondence (with its frequent quotations from the Bible and from Orthodox prayers and its lapses into an ecclesiastical Old Church Slavic style for purposes of either solemnity or irony) and in the religious themes of many of his short stories. The Russian clergy appear in Chekhov's stories as frequently as do other social groups. In this Chekhov differs markedly from Tolstoy and Dostoyevsky, who, for all their preoccupation with religion, never thought of making an Orthodox priest, deacon or monk a central character in a work of fiction as Chekhov did in "The Bishop," "On Easter Eve," "Saintly Simplicity," "A Nightmare" and so many other stories. Most of these men of the Church are presented as full-blooded human beings with their own joys and problems; but we also find in Chekhov an occasional mean, dehumanized cleric, such as the heartless priest who appears briefly toward the end of "In the Ravine" or the nasty and vicious one who provides the comic element in "It Was Not Fated."

Chekhov's own favorite among the hundreds of stories he wrote was "The Student," a very brief story that, in moving and utterly simple terms, states the case for the importance of religious traditions and

Excerpts from *Letters of Anton Chekhov* translated by Henry Heim, selection and introduction by Simon Karlinsky. Copyright (c) 1973 by Harper & Row, Publishers, Inc. Reprinted by permission of HarperCollins Publishers.

religious experience for the continuation of civilization. In Chekhov's last prose masterpiece, "The Bishop," the churchman-hero, sustained by his faith, faces the prospect of his own death with understanding and dignity, whereas a man much closer to Chekhov's own spiritual outlook, the professor of medicine in "A Dreary Story," who has no faith to lean on, deteriorates and withdraws from the life around him. The religious solace sought and found by Sonya in *Uncle Vanya* and by Yulia in "Three Years" are depicted by Chekhov with the utmost sympathy and understanding. And it was the nonbeliever Chekhov who, in the character of Lipa in "In the Ravine," created one of the most persuasive portraits of a meek Christian saint in Russian literature, comparable only to the similar creation of another nonbeliever, Turgenev's Lukeria in "The Living Relic."

Yet, for all these examples, religion, Christianity and the Church in Chekhov's work are totally divorced from the very things they are traditionally supposed to promote in Western civilization: morality, kindness and ethical treatment of fellow human beings. There are people in Chekhov's stories who are naturally good and kind, and religious belief or going to church are not shown to affect their natural goodness in one way or the other. But the unkind and the uncharitable in Chekhov's work, the exploiters and the manipulators, can and do use religion self-righteously and with impunity to further their selfish ends. The closest we come to an out-and-out villain in Chekhov's writings is the pious, churchgoing peasant Matvei in "Peasant Women," who uses religious teachings and prayers to rid himself of the woman he has seduced, to betray her, to frame her for a crime she probably did not commit and, after her death, to exploit and terrorize her small son. Another churchgoing Christian, the shopkeeper Andrei in "The Requiem," condemns his actress daughter as a harlot and is enabled by his religious beliefs to persist in this condemnation even after his priest explains to him how wrong he is. A whole gallery of cultivated upper-class ladies in Chekhov's stories use their church-sanctioned positions as Christian wives and mothers to humiliate other human beings (the professor's wife in "A Dreary Story"), to assert their own smug superiority (Maria Konstantinovna in "The Duel") or to bludgeon another person into submission (the wife in "The Chorus Girl"). The wise old professor in "A Dreary Story" drives this point home when he remarks that "virtue and purity are little different from vice when they are practiced in the spirit of unkindness."

While Tolstoy and Dostoyevsky both believed that Christian faith was the main source of moral strength for the impoverished and ignorant Russian peasants, Chekhov's much more closely observed and genuinely experienced picture of peasant life shows nothing of the sort. In the poverty-ridden world of "The Peasants," religion and the Church do nothing whatsoever to raise the moral or ethical level of the benighted peasantry, whose religious expression takes the form of superstition or of empty and meaningless ritual (this story so contradicted everything Tolstoy believed about Russian peasant religiosity that he called it a "sin against the Russian people"). In Chekhov's most brutal and violent story, "Murder," a family of peasant religious fanatics are led by their search for God to hate and brutalize each other and to commit a religiously motivated murder.

In a literature that had produced Gogol, Tolstoy, Dostoyevsky and Leskov, the view that Christianity and religion in general are morally neutral is startling enough. This view is clearly subversive from the point of view of all established churches, but Chekhov's simultaneous insistence that religious experience can be tremendously enriching and rewarding when it brings consolation and spiritual profundity into people's lives sits very badly with his Soviet commentators and annotators, who are duty-bound to represent all religion as exploitative and reactionary. Chekhov's view of sex, however, is even more startling, coming as it does from a writer raised in the second half of the nineteenth century. For Chekhov, sex, like religion, is also a morally neutral quantity, whose moral and ethical implications depend on the circumstances and the attitudes of the people involved. Had Chekhov stated such a view openly and militantly in the midst of the Victorian age in which he was living, he would have been dismissed as a crackpot by almost everyone. Because of his usual gentle and subdued mode of presentation, he was able to make his point without shocking too many people—but it was at the cost of having his views in this area almost overlooked.

In the eighteenth century, and especially during the reign of Catherine the Great, Russian literature enjoyed considerable freedom in treating sexual themes. Alexander Pushkin, who was the last nineteenth-century Russian writer to have profound ties with eighteenth-century traditions, was also the last to write openly and without guilt about the joys of sexual love. Pushkin's remarkably free treatment of sexual themes . . . was no longer possible when the long night of Victorian repression of all sexuality descended on Russia, as it did on other European countries. . . .

Of course, Anton Chekhov was a man of his time. He did not try to write of sexual love with the same freedom that Pushkin enjoyed and that he himself occasionally displayed in his private letters (making some of them unpublishable in Russian to this day). Nor could he permit himself the open treatment of the less-usual forms of sexuality which had been possible in the eighteenth century and became briefly possible again in the first two decades of the twentieth for certain Russian writers of the Symbolist period. But his ideal of the utmost literary objectivity prevented him from overlooking this basic human drive, from substituting the subjectively desirable in this sphere for that which actually exists, and from imposing moralizing sanctions and inflicting morally motivated penalties on his "transgressing" (i.e., sexually liberated) characters, as had been the custom in the literature of his time.

In 1886, the year that marks Chekhov's attainment of full literary maturity, he wrote four masterful stories that show young women of various social strata in out-of-wedlock sexual involvements. In "Agafya," the young peasant wife of a railroad switchman is caught by her husband when she fails to return in time from a tryst with her lover; "Anyuta" is about an urban proletarian girl, who cohabits with a succession of university students; "The Chorus Girl" is another lower-class woman, active as a call girl in addition to her job as an entertainer; and in "A Calamity," the wife of a well-to-do lawyer discovers hitherto unsuspected sexual desires within herself when an old family friend suddenly starts pursuing her with his attentions. What interested Chekhov in these stories is not that his heroines are having sexual experiences not sanctioned by the morality of the times, but rather what is done to them by others and what they do to themselves in connection with these experiences. Agafya comes to grief not because she has betrayed her husband, but because she needs her lover more than he needs her and because he refuses to take an interest in the consequences for her of their involvement. Anyuta is shown as an appealing, almost saintly creature, whose educated temporary lover is too tied down by social prejudices and cultural stereotypes to appreciate her selfless kindness. The same prejudices and stereotypes, mechanically accepted by everyone involved, enable the client and his self-dramatizing, bitchy wife to subject the heroine of "The Chorus Girl" to undeserved humiliation and actually to rob her, with her own guilty compliance, of her few pieces of jewelry. And, while Sofya in "A Calamity" finds her newly discovered sexuality alarming and distateful, it is because her discovery brings out the discrepancy between the bourgeois wife and mother she thinks herself to be and her true self, and also because her sexual drive becomes obsessive, robbing her of the ability to decide freely on a course of action.

The very concepts of "adultery," "adultress," "the fallen woman," so very important in Russian literature of the Victorian age, simply do not exist as far as Chekhov is concerned. The fact that a man and a woman not married to each other may sleep together has no moral or immoral dimensions or value in his stories and plays. When sex is degrading in Chekhov (as it is in "A Calamity" or in "Ariadne"), it is because the people involved have degraded it, not because degradation is intrinsic to it as it so often is in Dostoyevsky. Nor does Chekhov accept the facile notion, made popular by Dobrolyubov in his celebrated essay on Ostrovsky's play *The Thunderstorm*, that in tsarist Russia marital infidelity could be a form of social protest. Even though the educated heroines of "The Duel" and "An Unknown Man's Story" tend to regard themselves as socially and politically liberated because they have left their husbands and are openly living with their lovers, Chekhov gently exposes their attitudes as wishful illusions, stemming from the same set of taboos and prohibitions that would have branded them "adultresses" or "fallen women" in the work of most of his contemporaries.

Chronology

1860   Anton Chekhov born 29 January in Taganrog on the Sea of Azov, third son of a grocery merchant and grandson of a serf.

1876   Father and family flee to Moscow to escape bankruptcy proceedings: Anton lives on at family home, which has been sold, tutoring to support himself. Continues school at Taganrog Gymnasium.

1879   Graduates in July from Taganrog Gymnasium with city fellowship to University of Moscow Medical School, which he begins in September. Lives with and supports family.

1880   Publishes first story, "The Letter from the Don Landowner Stephan Vladimirovich N. to his Learned Neighbor Dr. Frederick," in March. Nine other stories published, including "Because of Little Apples." Writes long untitled play (*Platonov*) which is rejected for production and not published until after his death.

1881   Publishes regularly in various humorous magazines, including *Alarm Clock* (*Budilnik*) and *Spectator* (*Zritel*).

1882   Publishes in St. Petersburg entertainment weekly *Fragments* (*Oskolki*), now his preferred publishing outlet as he begins relationship with its editor Leykin.

1883   Writes regular column "Fragments of Moscow Life" for *Fragments*. Assistant at rural hospital in summer.

1884   Graduates from Medical School. Publishes mystery novel, *The Shooting Party*, and first collection of stories, *Tales of Melpomene*. Total of 250 items published since 1880.

1885   Begins publishing regularly in *St. Petersburg Gazette* (*Petersburgskaya gazeta*), now his preferred publishing outlet. Publishes "The Huntsman."

1886   Publishes "Misery." Begins publishing in *New Times* (*Novoye vremya*) under his own name with "The Requiem," "The Witch," and "Agafya," and pursues relationship with editor Suvorin; this newspaper, the largest in Russia, now his preferred publishing outlet. Publishes "Easter Eve," "Dreams," and "Vanka." Second collection, *Motley Tales*, will go through additional editions in later years.

1887 Publishes "The Kiss" and two more collections, *In the Twilight* (which goes through many editions in subsequent years) and *Innocent Speeches*. Produces initial draft of first mature play *Ivanov*.

1888 Publishes "Sleepy." "The Steppe" is first publication in serious literary journal, *The Northern Herald*. Awarded Pushkin Prize. Publishes another collection, *Tales*, and "The Party."

1889 Publishes another collection, *Children*, and "A Dreary Story." Writes unsuccessful play *The Wood Demon*.

1890 Publishes "Thieves" and another collection, *Gloomy People*. Travels to Sakhalin Island overland through Siberia; returns by boat via Hong Kong and Ceylon. Publishes "Gusev."

1891 Publishes "The Duel." Takes six-week tour of Europe, including Vienna, Rome, Paris. Participates in famine relief. Begins work on nonfiction book about Sakhalin Island, which takes over two years to complete.

1892 Publishes "The Butterfly"; "Ward Number Six." Buys small estate Melikhovo, where he lives with his father, mother and sister for a half dozen very productive years. Continues to practice medicine.

1893 Publishes "An Anonymous Story." *The Island: A Journey to Sakhalin* completed.

1894 Publishes "A Woman's Kingdom" and "Rothschild's Fiddle." Publishes another collection, *Stories and Tales*.

1895 Publishes "Three Years." Meets Tolstoy. Publishes "The Order of St. Anne" and "Ariadne." Completes initial draft of play *The Seagull*.

1896 Publishes "The Artist's Story"; and "My Life." Builds peasant school.

1897 Suffers serious hemorrhage from tuberculosis. Publishes "Peasants," "In the Cart," and the play *Uncle Vanya*, a rewrite of earlier *The Wood Demon* (1889). Visits Europe.

1898 Publishes informal trilogy: "A Hard Case," "Concerning Love," and "Gooseberries." Father dies. Moscow performance of *The Seagull* establishes reputation as playwright.

1899 Publishes "Angel." Moves to Yalta for health. Begins revisions of early stories for edition of collected works. Meets Gorky. Publishes "A Lady with a Dog."

1900 Publishes "In the Hollow." Elected to Academy of Sciences, literature division. Publishes initial draft of play *The Three Sisters*. Relationship with Olga Knipper, an actress in his plays, deepens. Health continues to deteriorate.

1901 Marries Olga Knipper. First collected works published.

1902 Publishes "The Bishop." Resigns Academy of Sciences in protest of Gorky's exclusion for political reasons.

1903 Publishes "A Marriageable Girl"; completes play *The Cherry Orchard* despite physical weakness from advanced stage of tuberculosis.

1904 Dies at Badenweiler, Germany, 2 July.

Appendix of Russian Titles and Alternate Title Translations

This appendix is alphabetized according to the translated titles used in the text. Russian titles appear directly after, followed by their dates of publication. Alternate English titles appear beneath the original Russian title.

"An Actor's End"
  "Atyorskaya gibel" 1886

"Agafya"
  "Agatha" 1886

"All Friends Together"
  "U znakomykh" 1898
  "A Visit to Friends"

"Angel"
  "Dushechka" 1898
  "The Darling"

"An Anonymous Story"
  "Rasskaz neizvestnogo cheloveka" 1893
  "Tale of an Unknown Man"

"Anyuta"
  "Anyuta" 1886

"Ariadne"
  "Ariadna" 1895

"Art"
  "Khudozhestvo" 1886
  "Artistry"

"The Artist's Story"
  "Dom s mezoninom—Rasskaz khudozhnika" 1896
  "The House With a Mansard—An Artist's Story"
  "The House With the Mezzanine"
  "The House With the Attic"

"At Sea—A Sailor's Story"
  "V more—Rasskaz matrosa," 1883

"At the Mill"
  "Na melnitse" 1886

"An Avenger"
  "Mstitel" 1887

"An Awkward Business"
  "Nepriyatnost" 1888
  "An Unpleasant Business"
  "An Unpleasantness"
  "A Trivial Matter"

"The Baron"
  "Baron" 1882

"The Beggar"
  "Nishchy" 1887

"The Bet"
  "Pari" 1888

"The Bishop"
  "Arkhiyerey" 1902

"The Black Monk"
  "Chorny Monakh"

"Boys"
  "Malchiki" 1887

"The Butterfly"
    "Poprygunya" 1892
    "The Grasshopper"
    "La Cigale"

"Calchas"
    "Kalkhas" 1886

"A Case History"
    "Sluchay iz praktiki" 1898
    "A Doctor's Visit"

"A Chameleon"
    "Khameleon" 1884

"The Chemist's Wife"
    "Aptekarsha" 1886
    "The Young Wife"

"Children"
    "Detvora" 1886

"The Chorus Girl"
    "Khoristka" 1886

"Concerning Love"
    "O lyubvi" 1898
    "About Love"

"The Conqueror's Triumph"
    "Torzhestvo pobeditelya" 1883
    "Victor's Triumph"

"A Cook's Wedding"
    "Kukharka zhenitsya" 1885

"Darkness"
    "Temnota" 1887

"A Daughter of Albion"
    "Doch Albiona," 1883

"A Day in the Country"
  "Den za gorodom" 1886

"The Death of a Government Clerk"
  "Smert chinovnika," 1883

"The Dependents"
  "Nakhlebniki" 1886

"Difficult People"
  "Tyazholye lyudi" 1886

"Dr. Startsev"
  "Ionych" 1898
  "Ionitch"

"Dreams"
  "Mechty" 1886

"A Dreary Story—From An Old Man's Memoirs"
  "Skuchnaya istoriya—Iz zapisok starovo cheloveka" 1889
  "A Boring Story"
  "A Tedious Story"
  "A Tiresome Story"

"Drowning"
  "Utoplennik—Stsenka" 1885
  "The Drowned Man—A Sketch"

"Drunk"
  "Pyanye" 1887

"The Duel"
  "Duel" 1891

"Easter Eve"
  "Svyatoyu Nochyu" 1886
  "On Easter Eve"
  "On Easter Night"

"An Encounter"
  "Vstrecha" 1887
  "The Meeting"

"An Endless Process"
  "Kanitel" 1885

"Enemies"
  "Vragi" 1887
  "Two Tragedies"

"An Enigmatic Nature"
  "Zagadochnaya natura" 1883

"Excellent People"
  "Khoroshiye lyudi" 1886

"Fat and Thin"
  "Tolstoi i tonki" 1883
  "Lean and Fat"

"A Father"
  "Otets" 1887

"A Gentleman Friend"
  "Znakomy muzhchina" 1886
  "An Acquaintance"

"Gooseberries"
  "Kryzhovnik" 1898

"Green Scythe"
  "Zelyonaya kosa—Malenky roman" 1882
  "The Village of Green Scythe—A Little Novel"
  "Green Point"

"Grisha"
  "Grisha" 1886

"Gusev"
  "Gusev" 1890

"Happiness"
  "Shastye" 1887

"A Hard Case"
  "Chelovek v futlyare" 1898
  "The Man in a Case"
  "The Man in a Shell"

"He Understood"
  "On ponyal," 1883

"Home"
  "V rodnom uglu" 1897
  "At Home"

"Home"
  "Doma" 1887
  "At Home"

"The Huntsman"
  "Yeger" 1885
  "The Gamekeeper"

"The Husband"
  "Muzh" 1886

"Hush"
  "Tsss!" 1886

"In Exile"
  "V ssylke" 1892

"In Spring"
  "Vesnoy" 1886

"In the Autumn"
  "Osenyu" 1883

"In the Cart"
  "Na podvode" 1897
  "A Journey by Cart"
  "The Schoolmistress"

"In the Dark"
   "V poryomkakh" 1886

"In the Graveyard"
   "Na kladbischche" 1884
   "In the Cemetery"

"In the Hollow"
   "V ovrage" 1900
   "In the Ravine"

"In the Home for the Senile and the Incredibly Ill"
   "Vi priyute dlya neizlechimo-bolynkh i pretarelykh," 1884

"Ivan Matveyitch"
   "Ivan Matveyitch" 1886

"The Jeune Premier"
   "Pervy lyubovnik" 1886

"A Joke"
   "Shutochka" 1886

"Kashtanka—A Story"
   "Kashtanka—Razzkaz" 1887

"The Kiss"
   "Potseluy" 1887

"The Lady of the Manor"
   "Barynya" 1882
   "The Mistress"
   "The Baroness"

"A Lady With A Dog"
   "Dama s sobachkoy" 1899
   "The Lady With the Pet Dog"

"Late-Blooming Flowers"
   "Tzvety zapozdalye" 1882

"Late Flowers"
"Belated Blossoms"

"The Letter"
"Pismo" 1887

"The Liberal—A New Year's Day Story"
"Liberal—Novogodny rasskaz" 1884
"The Radical"

"Lights"
"Ogni" 1888

"A Living Chattel"
"Zhivoy tovar" 1882
"Living Merchandise"
"Living Goods"
"Wife for Sale"

"The Lottery Ticket"
"Vyigryshny bilet" 1887

"Love"
"Lyubov" 1886

"A Malefactor"
"Zloumyshlennik" 1885
"A Culprit"
"A Miscreant"

"Mari d'Elle"
"Mari d'Elle" 1885

"A Marriageable Girl"
"Nevesta" 1903
"Betrothed"
"The Bride"

"The Mediocrities"
"Obyvateli" 1899
"The Philistines"

"Mire"
  "Tina" 1886

"Misery"
  "Toska" 1886
  "Heartache"
  "Grief"
  "The Lament"

"A Misfortune"
  "Neschastye" 1886
  "A Calamity"

"Moral Superiority"
  "Oba luchshe" 1885

"Murder"
  "Ubiystvo" 1895

"My Life—A Provincial's Story"
  "Moya Zhizn—Rasskaz provintsiala" 1896

"My Wife"
  "Zhena" 1892

"Neighbors"
  "Sosedi" 1892

"Nerves"
  "Nervy" 1885

"A Nervous Breakdown"
  "Pripadok" 1888
  "An Attack of Nerves"
  "A Fit"
  "The Seizure"

"The New Villa"
  "Novaya dacha" 1899

"Peasants"
  "Muzhiki" 1897

"A Nightmare"
  "Koshmar" 1886
  "An Incubus"

"Not Wanted"
  "Lishniye lyudi" 1886

"Old Age"
  "Starost" 1885

"On Official Business"
  "Po delam sluzhby" 1899
  "On Official Duty"

"On the Road"
  "Na puti" 1886
  "On the Way"

"The Orator"
  "Orator" 1886

"The Order of Saint Anne"
  "Anna na sheye" 1895
  "Anna on the Neck"

"Oysters"
  "Ustritsy" 1884

"The Party"
  "Imeniny" 1888
  "The Birthday Party"
  "Name-Day"

"Patch"
  "Belolody" 1895
  "Whitebrow"
  "Whitestar"

"Peasant Women"
  "Baby" 1891
  "Peasant Wives"

"A Pink Stocking"
  "Rosovy chulok" 1886

"The Pipe"
  "Svirel" 1887
  "The Shepherd's Pipe"
  "The Reed"

"A Play"
  "Drama" 1887

"The Privy Councillor"
  "Tayny sovetnik" 1886

"The Requiem"
  "Panikhida" 1886
  "Mass for the Sinner"

"The Retired Slave"
  "Otstavnoy rab," 1883

"Rothschild's Fiddle"
  "Skripka Rotschilda" 1894

"The Runaway"
  "Beglets" 1887
  "The Fugitive"

"The Russian Master"
  "Uchitel slovesnosti" 1894
  "The Teacher of Literature"

"St. Peter's Day"
  "Petrov den" 1882

"The Savage"
  "Pecheneg" 1897
  "The Petchenyeg"

"The Schoolmaster"
  "Uchitel" 1886

"Sergeant Prishibeyev"
  "Unter Prishibeyev" 1885

"The Sinner from Toledo—A Translation from the Spanish"
  "Greshnik iz Toledo—Perevod s ispanskovo" 1882
  "The Toledo Sinner"

"A Slander"
  "Kleveta" 1883
  "A Scandal Monger"

"Sleepy"
  "Spat khochetsya" 1888
  "Let Me Sleep"
  "Sleepyhead"

"Sorrow"
  "Gore" 1885
  "Grief"
  "Woe"

"The Steppe: The Story of a Journey"
  "Step—Istoriya odnoy poyezdki"

"A Story Without an End"
  Rasskaz bez kontsa" 1886

"The Student"
  "Student" 1894

"The Swedish Match—A Murder Story"
  "Shvedskaya Spichka—Ugolovny roman" 1882

"Talent"
  "Talent" 1886

"A Theatre Manager Under the Sofa"
  "Antrepenyor pod divanom" 1885

"The Thief"
  "Vor" 1883

"Thieves"
  "Vory" 1889
  "The Horse-Stealers"

"Three Years"
  "Tri Goda" 1894

"A Trifle From Life"
  "Zhiteyskaya meloch" 1886
  "A Trifling Occurrence"

"Trifon"
  "Trifon" 1884

"A Trivial Incident"
  "Pustoy sluchay" 1886

"The 29th of June—The Story of a Huntsman Who Never Hit Any-thing"
  "Dvadsat devyatoye iyun—Rasskaz okhotnika nikogda v tsel nye popadayushchevo" 1882

"Two in One"
  "Dvoye v odnom" 1883

"Typhus"
  "Tif" 1887

"An Upheaval"
  "Perepolokh" 1886

"Uprooted—An Incident of My Travels"
  "Perekati pole—Putevoy nabrosok" 1887
  "The Rolling Stone—A Traveller's Sketch"
  "Thistledown"

"Vanka"
  "Vanka" 1886

"Verotchka"
  "Verotchka" 1887

"The Village Elder"
  "Starosta—Stsenka" 1886

"Volodya"
  "Volodya" 1887

"Ward Number Six"
  "Palata No 6" 1892

"The Witch"
  "Vedma" 1886

"The Woman Who Had No Prejudices—A Romance"
  "Zhenshchina bez predrassudkov—Roman" 1883
  "An Unprejudiced Girl—A Love Story"

"A Woman's Kingdom"
  "Babye tsarstvo" 1894

"Women Make Trouble"
  "Ty i by—Stsenka" 1886
  "Thou and You"

"Worse and Worse"
  "Iz ognya da v polymya" 1884

Selected Bibliography

Primary Works

Translations of Short Fiction

Note: I have listed the translations cited in this book. For a more complete list of translations, with 36 entries by 26 translators noted in chronological order, see Constance Garnett's *Tales of Chekhov*, vol. 13, 339–341.

Chertok, I. C., and Jean Gardner, trans. *Late-Blooming Flowers and Other Stories.* New York: Carroll and Graf, 1964.

Dunnigan, Ann, trans. *Selected Stories.* New York: New American Library, 1960.

FitzLyon, April, and Kyril Zinovieff, trans. *The Woman in the Case and Other Stories.* London: Spearman and Calder, 1953.

Garnett, Constance, trans. *The Tales of Chekhov.* 13 vols. New York: Macmillan, 1917–23; rpt. New York: Ecco Press, 1984–87. Vol. 13 includes a title index.

Hinchcliffe, Arnold, trans. *The Sinner from Toledo and Other Stories.* Rutherford, New Jersey: Fairleigh Dickinson University Press, 1972.

Hingley, Ronald, trans. and ed. *The Oxford Chekhov.* Vol. 4–9. London: Oxford University Press, 1965–1980.

Jones. *St. Peter's Day and Other Tales.* Translated by Frances H. Jones. New York: Capricorn Books (Copyright: G. P. Putnam's Sons), 1959.

Miles. *Chekhov: The Early Stories, 1883–1888.* Translated by Patrick Miles and Harvey Pitcher. New York: Macmillan Publishing Co., 1982.

Miller. *Anton Chekhov: Collected Works in Five Volumes: Volume One: Stories 1880–1885.* Translated by Alex Miller and Ivy Litvinov (other translators listed at the end of some stories). Edited by Raissa Bobrova. Moscow: Raduga Publishers, 1967.

Payne. *The Image of Chekhov: Forty Stories by Anton Chekhov in the Order in Which They Were Written.* Translated by Robert Payne. New York: Vintage, 1966. Reprinted by arrangement with Alfred A. Knopf; copyright 1963 by Alfred A. Knopf.

Smith. *The Thief and Other Tales.* Translated by Ursula Smith. New York: The Vantage Press, 1964.

Yarmolinsky 1947. *The Portable Chekhov.* (Stories used in this text translated by Yarmolinsky.) Edited by Avrahm Yarmolinsky. New York: The Viking

Press, 1947. (Note: reference to Chekhov's letters are not from this source, but from *Letters of Anton Chekhov*, ed. Avrahm Yarmolinsky. See Bibliography, "Letters" below.)

Yarmolinsky 1954. *The Unknown Chekhov: Stories and Other Writings hitherto Untranslated.* Translated with an Introduction by Avrahm Yarmolinsky. New York: The Noonday Press, 1954. (Note: references to Chekhov's letters are not from this source, but from *Letters of Anton Chekhov*, ed. Avrahm Yarmolinsky. See Bibliography, "Letters" below.)

Collected Works in Russian

Belchikov, N. F., et al, eds. *Polnoye sobraniye sochineny i pisem v tridsati tomakh.* 30 vols. Moscow, 1974–83.

Balukhaty, S. D., et al, eds. *Polnoye sobraniye sochineny i pisem v dvenadtsati tomakh.* 20 vols. Moscow, 1944–51.

Letters

Anton Chekhov's Life and Thought: Selected Letters and Commentary. Translated by Michael Heim with Simon Karlinsky; selection, commentary and introduction by Simon Karlinsky. Originally published as *Letters of Anton Chekhov.* New York: Harper and Row, 1973. Rpt. Berkeley: University of California Press, 1975.

Letters of Anton Chekhov. Selected and edited by Avrahm Yarmolinsky. New York: Viking Press, 1973.

Letters of Anton Chekhov to His Family and Friends with Biographical Sketch. Trans. Constance Garnett. New York: Macmillan, 1920.

Letters on the Short Story, the Drama, and Other Literary Topics. Selected and ed. Louis S. Friedland, with a Preface by Ernest Simmons. New York: Minto Beach, 1924; rpt. New York: Benjamin Blom, 1964.

The Life and Letters of Anton Tchekhov. Trans. and ed. S.S. Koteliansky and Philip Tomlinson. Cassell &Co. Ltd., London, 1925; rpt: New York: Benjamin Blom, 1965.

The Selected Letters of Anton Chekhov. Translated by Sidonie K. Lederer; edited with an Introduction by Lillian Hellman. New York: Farrar, Straus and Giroux, Inc., 1984.

Plays

The Oxford Chekhov. Vol. 1–3. Edited and translated by Ronald Hingley. London: Oxford University Press, 1964–1967. Vol. 1: *Short Plays.* Vol. 2: *Uncle Vanya, Three Sisters, The Cherry Orchard,* and *The Wood-Demon.* Vol. 3: *Platonov, Ivanov,* and *The Seagull.*

Selected Bibliography

Nonfiction

The Island: A Journey to Sakhalin. Translated by Luba and Michael Terpak. Introduction by Robert Payne. New York: Washington Square Press, 1967.

Secondary Works

Buford, Walter H. *Chekhov and His Russia: A Sociological Study.* 2d. ed., London: Routledge and Kegan Paul, 1948; rpt. Hamden, Conn.: Archon Books, 1971.

Chudakov, A. P. *Chekhov's Poetics.* Translated by Edwina Cruise and Donald Dragt. Ann Arbor: Ardis, 1983.

Clyman, Toby W., ed. *A Chekhov Companion.* Westport, Conn.: Greenwood Press, 1985.

Eekman, Thomas, ed. *Anton Cechov 1860–1960: Some Essays.* Leiden: Brill, 1960.

Eekman, Thomas, ed. *Critical Essays on Anton Chekhov.* Boston: G. K. Hall, 1989.

Halunciski, Leo and David Savignac, trans. and eds. *Anton Chekhov as a Master of Story-Writing: Essays in Modern Soviet Literary Criticism.* The Hague: Mouton, 1976.

Hahn, Beverly. *Chekhov: A Study of the Major Stories and Plays.* Cambridge: Cambridge University Press, 1977.

Hingley, Ronald. *A New Life of Anton Chekhov.* New York: Knopf, 1976.

Jackson, Robert Louis, ed. *Chekhov: A Collection of Critical Essays.* Englewood Cliffs, New Jersey: Prentice-Hall, 1967.

Kirk, Irina. *Anton Chekhov.* Boston: Twayne, 1981.

Kramer, Karl. *The Chameleon and the Dream: The Image of Reality in Cexov's Stories.* The Hague: Mouton, 1970.

Meister, Charles W. *Chekhov Criticism: 1880 Through 1986.* Jefferson, North Carolina: McFarland and Company, Inc., 1988.

McConkey, James, ed. *Chekhov and Our Age.* Ithaca, New York: Cornell University, n.d.

Rayfield, Donald. *Chekhov: The Evolution of His Art.* New York: Barnes and Noble, 1975.

Simmons, Ernest J. *Chekhov: A Biography.* Boston: Little Brown, 1962.

Stowell, H. Peter. *Literary Impressionism, James and Chekhov.* Athens, Ga.: University of Georgia Press, 1980.

Tulloch, John. *Chekhov: A Structuralist Study.* New York: Harper & Row, 1980.

Welleck, Rene and Nonna D. Welleck, eds. *Chekhov: New Perspectives.* Englewood Cliffs, New Jersey: Prentice-Hall, 1984.

Williames, Lee J. *Anton Chekhov: The Iconoclast.* Scranton, Pa.: University of Scranton Press, 1989.

Winner, Thomas. *Chekhov and His Prose.* New York: Holt, Rhinehart and Winston, 1966.

Yermilov, Vladimir. *Anton Pavlovich Chekhov, 1860–1904.* Trans. Ivy Litvinov.

Moscow: Foreign Language Publishing House, n.d.[1956]. (Russian original: Moscow, 1953.)

Bibliographies

"Bibliographical Index to the Complete Works of Anton Chekhov." In David Magarshack, *Chekhov: A Life*. New York: Grove Press, 1953; rpt. Westport, Conn.: Greenwood Press, 1970. 393–423.

"Chekhov's Stories: A Chronology." *Tales of Chekhov*, vol. 13, 345–350.

Leighton, Lauren. "Chekhov's Works in English: Selective Collections and Editions." In *A Chekhov Companion*, edited by Toby W. Clyman. 306–309.

Lantz, Kennth. *Anton Chekhov: A Reference Guide to Literature*. Boston: Mass.: G. K. Hall, 1985.

Heifitz, Anna. *Chekhov in English: A List of Works By and About Him*. Ed. with a foreword by Avrahm Yarmolinsky. New York: New York Public Library, 1948.

Yachnin, Rissa. *Chekhov in English: A Selective List of Works By and About Him 1949–1960*. New York: New York Public Library, 1960.

Index

Abrahams, William, 106–7n29
Anderson, Sherwood, x
Art of the Tale, The: An International Anthology of Short Stories 1945–1985 (Halpern, ed.), x

Babel, Isaac, x
Bunin, Ivan, 4, 101; *Memories and Portraits*, 111

Carver, Raymond, x, 76, 106–7n29; "Errand," 107n29
Catherine the Great, 133
Cheever, John, 21
Chekhov, Alexander, 3, 113–14, 131
Chekhov, Anton: adultery theme in works of, 19, 27–31; art stories of, 44–45; authentic life stories of, 84–96; bureaucracy theme in works of, 7–8; characterization in works of, xi–xii, 50, 62, 127–28; child theme in works of, 37–39; choice of genre by, 126–27; comedy stories of, 18–21; comic realism of, 13–15, 20–21, 106n28; and conservation, 41; criticism of Gorky by, 118–20; domestic theme in works of, 18–19, 21–24; Gothic influence on, 13, 19, 72–73; holiday stories of, 8–9, 59, 68–69, 102–3; human dignity theme in works of, 8–9, humor in works of, 5; inauthentic life theme in works of, 51–56, 58–62, 76–84; influence of, on short story, ix–xi, 106n23, 106–7n29; influence of Tolstoy on, 48, 105n15; isolation theme in works of, 25–27, 53–54; journalistic career of, 3–4; letters of, 112–21;

love theme in works of, 9–10, 24–27, 76–84; meaning of life in works of, 63–69, 128–29; medical influence on, 46–47, 65, 121; moral ambiguity in works of, 57–58; moral conversion of characters of, 65–66; narrative in, 21–22, 49, 76, 82, 127; naturalist influence on, 10, 34–35, 74–75; objectivity of, xiii, 15, 74; on being an artist, 114–115, 118; on writing about nature, 114, 119, 120; owning humans theme in works of, 9–12; parody in works of, 13–14; pathos in works of, 19–20; peasant stories of, 31–37, 74–75, 96–100, 132–33; perceived anti–semitism of, 30; as playwright, xii–xiii; and "prose–play," 33, 39–40, 44; psychological acuity in works of, 29, 59–61, 69, 70–71; relationship between the sexes in works of, 12–13; religious themes in works of, 41–44, 68–69, 100–103, 106n25, 131–33; secular humanism in, 94–96, 129–30; self–criticism of, 112–13; serious realism of, 15–16; setting in works of, xi, 18–19; significance of truth in works of, 93–94; spiritual dimension in, 68–69; stories of the elderly by, 39–41; and subjective *vs.* objective reality, 69–74; theatrical influences on, 13; theatrical themes of works of, 45–46; themes in works of, xii; theme of sex in works of, 133–35; translation of works of, xiii, xivn6; unfinished novel of, 126; use of

The Author

Ronald L. Johnson was born in Vancouver, Washington, in 1943, and has been fascinated with narrative for as long as he can remember. He completed a B.A. at California State University, Fresno, in 1967; an M.F.A. at the University of California, Irvine, in 1971, in fiction writing; and a Ph.D. at the University of Utah, in 1980. His dissertation, a novel, won first place in the Utah Arts Contest in 1981. He has published short fiction in small magazines in the United States and New Zealand, and has written reference articles for Salem Press. Currently, he teaches writing and literature at Northern Michigan University.